I've often been impressed with what happens during a crisis or disaster. People divide up into several types. Some stand there helplessly and just scream; they are like clueless children who literally have to be picked up and carried to a safe place. Others stampede out the door in order to save their own necks, even if it means killing someone who stands in their way. A few, however, have their wits about them. They are trying to keep their cool; they are trying to figure out the situation in the confusion. They formulate a plan not only to survive, but also to help others around them.

All three of those types sit beside you right now in your church. When times are good and secure, you have little idea of what is actually in your heart or the hearts of your fellow Christians. You don't know how you will react in a disaster. Only when our lives fall apart, when society, law and order, and health and wealth disintegrate around us, do we find out what we are really made of.

מָצָא אִשָּׁה מָצָא טוֹב וַיָּפֶק רָצוֹן מֵיְהוָה:

Proverbs 18:22

A Manual

for

Spiritual Survival

Dr. Charles R. Vogan Jr.

ISBN 978-0-6151-5902-7

Cover painting: **Ivan Aivazovsky** – *Shipwreck* (1876)

Many thanks to Don McCready and Jeremy Vogan for their editing help.

Ravenbrook Publishers

A subsidiary of
Shenandoah Bible Ministries

———— ᘯ ————

www.shenbible.org

1 2 **3**

4

Contents

Introduction

In this world you will have trouble. (John 16:33)

In times of hardship and disaster, when "the foundations are being destroyed," only the tough survive. Those who have become accustomed to a life of ease, security and prosperity don't know what to do when all that is forcibly ripped out of their lives. Since history shows us that disaster and hard times have a cyclical way of coming around to haunt us, only those who have the foresight to *prepare ahead of time* for what must inevitably come to pass will survive.

But in the typical church, there is almost no training going on. This is amazing, because Christian training is the *best* way to prepare for survival in hard times. The church is the only place where you can get those training resources and principles. Why aren't people using them to get ready? Probably because the current state of affairs in our society also rules in the church: a life of ease, prosperity and security (physically speaking!) seems more important than spiritual hardiness. This is the same problem that the Israelites had, which God had predicted of them.

> Be careful that you do not forget the LORD your God, failing to observe his commands, his laws and his decrees that I am giving you this day. Otherwise, when you eat and are satisfied, when you build fine houses and settle down, and when your herds and flocks grow large and your silver and gold increase and all you have is multiplied, then your heart will become proud and you will forget the LORD your God, who brought you out of Egypt, out of the land of slavery. (Deuteronomy 8:11-14)

The current church scene is anything but training. Pastors are more like salesmen and entertainers, struggling to keep people coming to the services instead of leaving to find more interesting "shows" elsewhere to please them. Christianity in the church has been reduced to doing *as little as possible*, because we don't want to pressure anybody and risk losing them. The leadership has almost backed completely away from confronting people with their sins and shortcomings, because that *would* chase them away. People don't come to church for the right reason – that they are sinners needing help. So, the real issues in their lives go unaddressed.

Now when society turns upside down, and people are persecuted by the government or their neighborhoods for being Christians, or disease and war rip up the fabric of everyday life, those problems underneath the surface that were not addressed at a superficial church service will come to the front. People *have* to get real answers then, because death and misery are right around the corner. They don't want to die unprepared. The problem is that bombs and firing squads and famine and the plague don't give us any time to research for answers. Millions will die while some of us try to figure out how to survive in such an upside-down world.

The time to prepare for such things is *now,* while we have the opportunity and the resources for preparation.

The point, however, is not to preserve as much of our physical possessions as we can. Christians ought to know that this isn't the point. Our calling is to establish a foothold on God's spiritual world, and rely less and less on this physical world. *That* is the secret to survival. If you can willingly give up the health and wealth and security of this world as they are taken from you, then how will it hurt you when you lose them?

> What is more, I consider everything a loss compared to the surpassing greatness of knowing Christ Jesus my Lord, for whose sake I have lost all things. I consider them rubbish *[the Greek word here is actually "dung"]*, that I may gain Christ and be found in him. (Philippians 3:8-9)

If you set your minds and hearts on things above, on Heavenly treasures, then the loss of this world's goods won't shake you as you hold out your hope for a better world.

But store up for yourselves treasures in Heaven, where moth and rust do not destroy, and where thieves do not break in and steal. For where your treasure is, there your heart will be also. (Matthew 6:20-21)

Get ready ahead of time

Some people plan for the future; they are the wise ones. Like the ant preparing for winter, they know that it's just a matter of time until trials and hardships come, and they do what they can *now* so that they will be ready. It means that they won't be able to play much now, but survival is more important to them than pleasure.

Others don't plan for the future at all. They want their good times now. Then, as the people in Noah's day found out, there is no time or opportunity to go back and fix what is broken when the disaster strikes.

As it was in the days of Noah, so it will be at the coming of the Son of Man. For in the days before the flood, people were eating and drinking, marrying and giving in marriage, up to the day Noah entered the ark; and they knew nothing about what would happen until the flood came and took them all away. That is how it will be at the coming of the Son of Man. (Matthew 24:37-39)

Hard times come because God sends them. I know that people bring it upon themselves; we build a house of cards out of our lives, so to speak, and then wonder why it all collapses around us at the worst time. But the Scripture says that God uses those catastrophes for his own ends: to judge the wicked, and to discipline his people. Only the pagans deny this, because they live in constant terror at the thought that such a God could rule over them in this way.

One nation was being crushed by another and one city by another, because God was troubling them with every kind of distress. (2 Chronicles 15:6)

Introduction

It's not a matter of *if* trials will happen, it's a matter of *when*. The wise understand this. The wise also know that the best way to be ready for trials and hardships in this world is *not* to build bunkers in your basement and change all your money into gold. The way to prepare is to *start learning the truth from Jesus* and build it into your life.

> Why do you call me, 'Lord, Lord,' and do not do what I say? I will show you what he is like who comes to me and hears my words and puts them into practice. He is like a man building a house, who dug down deep and laid the foundation on rock. When a flood came, the torrent struck that house but could not shake it, because it was well built.
>
> But the one who hears my words and does not put them into practice is like a man who built a house on the ground without a foundation. The moment the torrent struck that house, it collapsed and its destruction was complete. (Luke 6:46-49)

Ignore him at your peril! He knows the kind of foundation you will need when physical hardships happen: a *spiritual* foundation. You may not understand now how the two relate to each other, but you will later. The Creator knows that you need a spiritual Rock to stand on when the foundations of this world are swept away underneath you; it will happen to everybody, to God's people as well as to the wicked. There is no lasting hope in things in this world.

You must come to Jesus so that he can open up your heart and, like a doctor, cut that cancer out of you so that you will live. You *must* establish a relationship with God if you hope to survive. Your sinful flesh must be crucified, and you must start walking the road back to God, if you hope to live. It will seem hard to do this, giving up this world that you love so much so that you can lay claim to the next world; but it's a matter of discipline, and discipline is never easy.

> Anyone who does not take his cross and follow me is not worthy of me. Whoever finds his life will lose it, and whoever loses his life for my sake will find it. (Matthew 10:38-39)

No discipline seems pleasant at the time, but painful. Later on, however, it produces a harvest of righteousness and peace for those who have been trained by it. (Hebrews 12:11)

God doesn't owe this world anything, not when it wallows in rebellion, wickedness, murder, lust and idolatry. Anybody with "eyes to see" will know that disaster is lurking right around the corner. Men and nations have been destroyed all throughout history, not by natural forces but by the hand of God bringing them to the end of their ways. The more that people store up the wrath of God against them, the darker the storm clouds get, and the more concerned the people of God should become. It's time to look to our own souls and make sure that *we* are not the target of his wrath!

Since everything will be destroyed in this way, what kind of people ought you to be? You ought to live holy and godly lives as you look forward to the day of God and speed its coming. That day will bring about the destruction of the heavens by fire, and the elements will melt in the heat. But in keeping with his promise we are looking forward to a new Heaven and a new earth, the home of righteousness. So then, dear friends, since you are looking forward to this, make every effort to be found spotless, blameless and at peace with him. (2 Peter 3:11-14)

Notice what Peter says is the hot issue: "make every effort to be found spotless, blameless and at peace with him." Nobody will be able to hide themselves from God the Judge when he comes to uncover their hearts. The *righteous* will be saved (not the rich or the strong or the wise), and the wicked will be destroyed. God is going to separate his people from the chaff, and save them from the wrath to come.

The need for training

Living by faith isn't something that comes easy. When a person first becomes a Christian, he *wants* to live by faith, because of the new love he feels for God. But then begins the long training process to turn that desire into reality.

Churches are supposed to help the Christian learn this process. Unfortunately there is almost no training going on in churches. The most that people experience in church are the Sunday morning sermons and a weak "prayer meeting" during the week. Bible studies are more like opinion-sharing sessions. There are no tests given to measure spiritual progress; such a thing is unthinkable in the modern church (though tests are given all the time in the business and educational world!).

Until such time as the churches wake up to their duty of preparing Christians, we will have to resort to *self*-discipline. This is even harder, because most people find it much easier to train in the company of like-minded believers. It's almost impossible to find the time, or the inclination, to work on things by ourselves. *So it depends on how desperate you are to be a survivor.* It's up to you to follow this training program; you aren't going to find much help in others.

The reason that it's easier to train with others is because some Christians have been through those rough times already. They know what it will take to survive. Like a sergeant back from the front lines, he trains the recruits in the skills that he knows they will need out there on the battlefield. He saw what worked and what didn't work. He knows when the troops are ready. Never ask the troops themselves if they are ready! How would they know that? They want to quit long before they are good at doing anything; a person is naturally lazy when it comes to putting forth effort on goals he can't see. So, ask someone who has been in battle to measure their progress, and don't stop training them until *he* is satisfied that they are ready.

One huge problem that people have is that they think they will be equal to any situation *without training.* Do you remember your first attempt at riding a bicycle? It looked so easy! What a humiliation to get thrown down, and get gravel in your face and cuts on your knees. The fact that it took so long to master the thing gave us a new appreciation for those who could do it well. It turned out to be a hard-won skill.

The same goes for spiritual skills. Most Christians feel no need to train for them, because they are sure they can do what God requires of them when the time comes. They are fooling themselves. How many times, for example, has anger gotten the best of you when the situation that made you angry came upon you suddenly, without warning? Did you know that that *this was a test of the state of your heart?* What will you do when that situation lasts day after day, year after year, with no letup in sight? Will your anger turn into rage and murder, as it does with so many others? What *do* you have in your heart that you don't know about?

And training, as we shall see, involves hard work, continuous effort, hardship, measuring your progress, and getting better at things until you can do the job to God's satisfaction.

> But solid food is for the mature, who by constant use have *trained themselves* to distinguish good from evil. (Hebrews 5:14)

The survival of the church

The church is Christ's special agency on earth to help Christians reach their spiritual objective – namely, to live by faith in the Son of God. The resources are there, the Spirit is there, and the Lord himself rules over his people and blesses them with the treasures of Heaven. If you take advantage of this situation, you will come to church to learn to live with God, to crucify your sins, and cut your ties with the world. These are measurable objectives in a Christian's life, and the church is designed to help you.

Unfortunately not all churches understand the Mission. Even the leaders will change the functions of the church to cater to people's whims and fancies. Instead of sinners working on their problems, many people are in church to be entertained and do their "religious duty" on Sunday. They have no intention of working on their hearts. Try being specific sometime about what they intend to do about *their* sin and you will see what I mean! That's just getting too personal for most people; you will have war on your hands if you go there.

The church is supposed to be a spiritual hospital; as soon as we come inside, we are announcing to everyone that we are in need and we've come for help. Jesus said as much.

Introduction

> It is not the healthy who need a doctor, but the sick. I have not come to call the righteous, but sinners. (Mark 2:17)

At no time is this more needed than in times of disaster. Then you will find people waking up to the reality of their spiritual state – their great need of God, and the sin that is dragging them down with the world as it collapses under the judgment of God. The church in such times becomes a beacon, a fortress on the hill, a place of refuge for those seeking real help.

Just as individuals must train for times of disaster, so the church also must train and be ready. How are we going to change our churches from their present state to the "church militant?" Churches must wake up and change from being entertainment centers to training centers. If they refuse to do this, people in great spiritual need will turn away from such "blind guides" in disgust and look for real help elsewhere.

Training is the responsibility of the leaders. I'm sure that it's fear that keeps them from doing so. They are afraid that if they get tough and lead the people into discipline, they will lose a lot of the membership. Well, you've no doubt heard the saying that parents who indulge the whims of their children will get no respect from their children. The disciplinarians are respected and loved as *leaders* – those who can lead the members through hard times also. It takes wisdom to do that; any fool can be the Emcee at a party.

The leaders will need a special faith of their own to implement spiritual training programs in the church. Their faith enables them to minister to the sheep without regard to reputation or reward or man's approval. They aren't trying to "tickle the ears" of their hearers, but to lead them into life.

> Am I now trying to win the approval of men, or of God? Or am I trying to please men? If I were still trying to please men, I would not be a servant of Christ. (Galatians 1:10)

> Be shepherds of God's flock that is under your care, serving as overseers – not because you must, but because you

are willing, as God wants you to be; not greedy for money, but eager to serve. (1 Peter 5:2)

A church that is ready for whatever the future brings (and since we live in a dark world, it's guaranteed that it will include hard times) will have training and resources available to address the needs that people will have. It will be an efficient training center; the leaders will know how to direct people to God, and show them how to live by faith in God's spiritual world. The ministry will be efficient in isolating and dealing conclusively with sin. The church will be a great help in helping people sever their ties to the world, and welding them into God's family.

Not everyone will be ready

I've often been impressed with what happens during a crisis or disaster. People divide up into several types. Some stand there helplessly and just scream; they are like clueless children who literally have to be picked up and carried to a safe place. Others stampede out the door in order to save their own necks, even if it means killing someone who stands in their way. A few, however, have their wits about them. They are trying to keep their cool; they are trying to figure out the situation in the confusion. They formulate a plan not only to survive, but also to help others around them.

All three of those types sit beside you right now in your church. When times are good and secure, you have little idea of what is actually in your heart or the hearts of your fellow Christians. You don't know how you will react in a disaster. Only when our lives fall apart, when society, law and order, and health and wealth disintegrate around us, do we find out what we are really made of. Those who ignored the plea to train will simply stand there helplessly and scream, and go down with the chaos. Those who are only looking out for themselves will turn into Judases. Those who are already trained in the spiritual life, however, will not only survive the disaster but will be tremendous blessings to those whom they can reach.

God uses hardships to reveal the true state of our hearts. The real risk in trials is *not* losing what you have in this world, but losing your soul. The first thought of a true Christian is not, "How can I preserve my comfortable life?" But, "What is my standing before God?" *Am* I a Christian? Am I standing on the Rock from Heaven? Or am I fooling myself, and about to go down with the rest of the world as it collapses? In such times, God is revealing the true foundation under our feet. He has good reason for doing this, though it will be a very unpleasant experience.

Most people *have* been fooling themselves. They aren't standing on what they claim to be standing on. But only a storm that sweeps away the physical props under their feet will show this.

> If you falter in times of trouble, how small is your strength! (Proverbs 24:10)

> Examine yourselves to see whether you are in the faith; test yourselves. Do you not realize that Christ Jesus is in you – unless, of course, you fail the test? (2 Corinthians 13:5)

Is it too late?

Many won't even think about spiritual training until the need for it forces them to. Like the Israelites, why should they bother themselves with the disciplined life when they don't see any need for it? But when trouble comes, *everyone* "cries out to the Lord in their distress."

Is there hope in the middle of disaster that God will hear you and help you? There are two kinds of people who "cry out to the Lord in their distress." The first is the person who just wants God to take away the painful situation and give him back his blessings that he feels God owes him. For him there will be no answers or help from God.

> But since you rejected me when I called and no one gave heed when I stretched out my hand, since you ignored all my advice and would not accept my rebuke, I in turn will laugh at your disaster; I will mock when calamity overtakes you … Then they will call to me but I will not answer; they will look for me but will not find me. (Proverbs 1:24-26, 28)

The second person (while he also may at first blame God for letting this disaster happen to him) has had some time to suffer and think on it some more. Like Job, he comes to a change of mind – he gets a more humble attitude and approaches God with a new heart. The sinner repents; the servant submits; the enemy reconciles with the King. When the Israelites had some time to suffer and think about their sin, they came back to God humbled and repentant. *Then* God lifted their burdens and delivered them.

> Many times he delivered them, but they were bent on rebellion and they wasted away in their sin. But he took note of their distress when he heard their cry; for their sake he remembered his covenant and out of his great love he relented. (Psalm 106:43-45)

The wise man, however, sees trouble coming ahead of time and gets ready for it. When *he* goes to God for help, he isn't in a panic. He already trusts in God and he has no reason to fear whatever the enemy may throw at him. His soul is secure.

> A prudent man sees danger and takes refuge, but the simple keep going and suffer for it. (Proverbs 22:3)

> The fear of the LORD leads to life: Then one rests content, untouched by trouble. (Proverbs 19:23)

A practical training program

What we want to do here is address key areas that will prove to be invaluable assets in times of trouble, no matter what form that trouble may take. Each of these areas is vitally necessary for survival. If a soldier, for example, learned all the aspects of war but neglected to learn how to shoot a rifle, how long do you think he would survive on the battlefield? The day of reckoning *will* arrive and reveal his single weakness! The rest of his training will have amounted to nothing if he dies in front of the enemy unprepared. In the same way, a Christian can hardly call himself or herself spiritually prepared for any disaster if he or she ignores even one of these areas of training. And the more training, the better.

A survivor is able to do two things:

First, he knows how to walk by faith in God's spiritual world. God is real to him; Heaven, the spiritual world of God, is more precious to him than anything in this world.

> Whom have I in Heaven but you? And earth has nothing I desire besides you. My flesh and my heart may fail, but God is the strength of my heart and my portion forever. (Psalm 73:25-26)

If you can do this, it won't matter what is taken away from you, and it won't matter what happens to you. You're standing on a Rock that is above this world and its troubles. You already have all the life and joy and peace that you could possibly want in Christ.

> The LORD is my rock, my fortress and my deliverer; my God is my rock, in whom I take refuge. He is my shield and the horn of my salvation, my stronghold. (Psalm 18:2)

Second, you have to be able to cut your ties to this world when the time comes. And the time *will* come. You will lose health, wealth, family and friends, reputation, even your life; these things happen in hard times. But if you keep a light touch on this world, you won't panic when the time comes to give it up. You have something better to rest your heart on: God's world.

> And everyone who has left houses or brothers or sisters or father or mother or children or fields for my sake will receive a hundred times as much and will inherit eternal life. (Matthew 19:29)

At this point you may not know if you're able to do these two things. Most people don't know their hearts well enough to know for certain what they would do when the world around them collapses into chaos. They are used to living as a Christian in times of peace and prosperity, and they haven't yet been tested in the fire. Many, however, who thought they were standing firm will fall away when that fire comes. The key to survival is to assume that you *aren't* ready, and take seriously the warning that Jesus gave us to prepare for that day.

> See to it that you do not refuse him who speaks. If they did not escape when they refused him who warned them on earth, how much less will we, if we turn away from him who warns us from Heaven? At that time his voice shook the earth, but now he has promised, "Once more I will shake not only the earth but also the heavens." The words "once more" indicate the removing of what can be shaken – that is, created things – so that what cannot be shaken may remain. Therefore, since we are receiving a kingdom that cannot be shaken, let us be thankful, and so worship God acceptably with reverence and awe, for our "God is a consuming fire." (Hebrews 12:25-29)

To help you get ready, and to train you in these two spiritual skills, here are five areas that you can start working on to strengthen your faith.

- *Personal holiness* – Our connection with God is life; we have to understand how to stay in touch with God through good times and bad. There will be many times when that is our only hope, the only ray of light in a dark world. It will be the guiding light keeping us on the right path in the midst of confusion. The *way* we live day by day will be vitally important in times of trial.

- *Mastering the Bible* – The Bible is our training manual. It covers all the information that we will need to grow and survive spiritually. But it requires some skill and wisdom to mine the gold out of this book and get resources that will prove helpful in our struggle for survival.

- *Dealing with the Enemy* – Like it or not, we are in the middle of a war, which is why we have troubles in the first place. If you can see that, you will know why it's so important to identify our enemies, and to learn how to fight and win against them. There is no doubt that they are waging war against *you* – they are out to destroy you!

- ***Church work*** – The church is our haven, our source of resources and training, our brothers and sisters who share in our fight. We are responsible for our own souls, but the church is a crucial center of operations available to us. Plus we have obligations to our spiritual family there, to help them in their struggle. God put us together for a reason: to help each other survive.

- ***General discipline*** – Untrained employees or military recruits have little about them to insure success. Success requires some vital character traits, some strong habits, the ability to work with others, some wisdom in dealing with situations that separate the men from the boys, the sheep from the goats. The true Christian will "persevere to the end."

The Survivor

A disaster brings confusion and panic in its wake. People are thrown off-guard; they don't know what's going on, and they don't know what to do. This is, in fact, the goal of an enemy: to sow the seeds of confusion, mental darkness, and panic so that he will have an easy time manipulating you and destroying you.

The key to survival in any situation is being able to see what's really going on, to separate the facts from the confusion, and discover a path to take that will lead you safely through the situation. Not everybody can do this.

Spiritual survival, as we've mentioned already, is going to be your safeguard in *both* physical and spiritual disasters. Since God usually sends disaster on a nation or people to shake out the good from the bad, you're not going to be able to protect yourself from the physical side of the troubles. *Everyone* will suffer loss of some kind. The wicked will be destroyed, and God's people will be tested to see what foundation they are really standing on.

> All share a common destiny – the righteous and the wicked, the good and the bad, the clean and the unclean, those who offer sacrifices and those who do not. As it is with the good man, so with the sinner; as it is with those who take oaths, so with those who are afraid to take them. (Ecclesiastes 9:2)

But only those who have developed spiritual skills will survive the physical hardships. Unbelievers don't understand this; they try to safeguard their possessions or health when everyone around them is losing theirs. But Christians know that it's just a matter of time until disaster comes around to them, and they're working on securing a safe place to hide spiritually, in God, who alone will bring them safely through. There are more important issues here than physical comfort and wealth! One's soul is at stake.

So, Christians have the advantage here over everyone else. There are two things that they are able to do that carry them *on top* of the flood, like an Ark, instead of going under in despair. They have to go through the flood like everyone else, but instead of sinking, they float. They have a raft of two planks that carries them through.

Faith

The first plank in our survivor's raft is faith. But faith is not what some people think it is. Many think that faith means hoping that something is true, or wishing for it. "I believe that God wants me to ..." Or, "I believe that God is like ..." Where they got some of their ideas, I don't know. But they have no Biblical basis for that kind of faith.

The kind of faith that God gives his people sheds a new light on everything so that we can *see*. This is going to make the difference between survival and failure.

Let's start at the beginning. Man was originally designed to know God. He had the ability to live in two worlds: in this physical world with his physical senses, and in God's spiritual world with the senses of his spirit. He had to be able to get in touch with God, because of his calling.

> Then God said, "Let us make man in our image, in our likeness, and let them **rule** over the fish of the sea and the birds of the air, over the livestock, over all the earth, and over all the creatures that move along the ground." (Genesis 1:26)

Man was God's governor, so to speak, assigned the task of ruling over and maintaining God's creation. He had to follow God's will, so that the world would function the way God wanted it to function. Since God made a world that was "very good" (Genesis 1:31), it was man's job to make sure that it stayed "very good." And that required the ability to know God and know his will.

The Survivor

Sin, however, ruined everything. When man turned away from God and his will, God shut the door to Heaven (see Genesis 3) and isolated man in the darkness of his mind and heart. Now the entire human race is completely unable to know God. Keep in mind that knowing God is life (see John 17:3); so when God cut off access to his throne, man died spiritually. Adam passed this spiritual liability to all of his descendants, including you and me. We were all born dead spiritually.

The results of this spiritual death and blindness have been catastrophic. Not knowing how to maneuver safely in God's world, it seems that we are doomed to bring disaster on our heads at every turn. We can't do anything without hurting ourselves in some way. We murder and steal and lie, which only makes life infinitely more difficult for ourselves and others. Instead of a stable society we have chaos and lawlessness. We can't do the simplest things right.

> Furthermore, since they did not think it worthwhile to retain the knowledge of God, he gave them over to a depraved mind, to do what ought not to be done. They have become filled with every kind of wickedness, evil, greed and depravity. They are full of envy, murder, strife, deceit and malice. They are gossips, slanderers, God-haters, insolent, arrogant and boastful; they invent ways of doing evil; they disobey their parents; they are senseless, faithless, heartless, ruthless. Although they know God's righteous decree that those who do such things deserve death, they not only continue to do these very things but also approve of those who practice them. (Romans 1:28-32)

In such a world, *everyone* is doomed. There can be no survivors in a world like this. Not only are we destroying ourselves, God himself is also making sure that we all die. He can't allow such depraved and lawless creatures to run loose in his Kingdom.

The only hope we have is for God to have mercy on a few of us here and there and *lead us out of this mess*. And that, as a matter of fact, is the good news of the Gospel. Christ has come to show us the way to God, out of death and into life.

He does it by first turning the light on. As we mentioned earlier, the main characteristic of a disaster is the mental darkness and confusion that reigns over the battlefield. When we can't see what's gong on, chances are really good that we're just getting further and further into trouble, no matter which way we go. What we need is some light. We have to be able to see what's going on around us, and see a way of escape. Spiritually, this is called *living by faith*.

When a person is converted, the Spirit gives them life (2 Corinthians 3:6) from Heaven, and they wake up from the dead. They now have the ability to see and know God, as man was designed to do in the beginning. They now live in the light of God's spiritual world.

> For you were once darkness, but now you are light in the Lord. Live as children of light (for the fruit of the light consists in all goodness, righteousness and truth) and find out what pleases the Lord. Have nothing to do with the fruitless deeds of darkness, but rather expose them. For it is shameful even to mention what the disobedient do in secret. But everything exposed by the light becomes visible, for it is light that makes everything visible. This is why it is said: "Wake up, O sleeper, rise from the dead, and Christ will shine on you." Be very careful, then, how you live – not as unwise but as wise, making the most of every opportunity, because the days are evil. (Ephesians 5:8-16)

You can immediately see from this passage how important this light from Heaven is going to be for us. It shows us many things that we need to know:

- *God's glory* – We can see now who God is: he created us; we exist to serve him; he is the Judge who knows our hearts; he is the wisdom and power behind everything in Creation. God is the center of everything, the God of glory, the holy God, who alone deserves to be worshiped and enjoyed. We become God-centered instead of self-centered, and that's going to keep us headed in the right direction for a change. Now we know what we've been created for.

- *The dangers of sin* – When the light turns on from Heaven, we can see now why rebellion against God is so dangerous and destructive. This world was made a certain way; to twist it against God's purposes is to destroy it and ourselves in the process. Sin is deliberately disobeying the King, and dishonoring him. It's replacing the only good God with something else that we prefer instead of him. It's an insult to God. It's a cancer in our souls, a poison in all of our relationships, a sure and certain path to destruction and misery. Being able to see the truly deadly nature of this otherwise tempting sin will bring us to a halt, unwilling to enter this darkness.

- *The new life in Christ* – We have a way of escaping this world of death and destruction: union with Christ. He came to get us out of here. His plan is to take the human situation upon himself and solve it completely. He can't fail, so now a human being has returned to God alive and willing to live with God on God's terms. He provides the pattern that we will fit into. And he makes us one with him so that we can share in his new life. All we have to do is stay with him.

They say that "knowledge is power." This is so true in the spiritual world. Being able to see the truth will make all the difference in the battle for survival.

We have to train ourselves to walk by faith, not by sight.

The righteous will live by faith. (Romans 1:17)

We live by faith, not by sight. (2 Corinthians 5:7)

We know very well how to live by our physical senses, because we've been doing it since the day we were born. But precisely because we are so used to doing this, it will get in the way when we try to live by faith. Our sinful nature that finds comfort and pleasure in the physical world will wage war against the Spirit, who is leading us away from that same physical world toward God.

> Those who live according to the sinful nature have their minds set on what that nature desires; but those who live in accordance with the Spirit have their minds set on what the Spirit desires. (Romans 8:5)

This isn't going to be easy. As you may have discovered already in a disaster situation, we tend to panic; our minds and hearts run first to find a solution that will preserve body and possessions. That is *not* the answer; it's still rebelling against God. We are our own worst enemy in times of trouble; we actually aid the enemy in destroying ourselves. As Paul said in Romans –

> So I find this law at work: When I want to do good, evil is right there with me. For in my inner being I delight in God's Law; but I see another law at work in the members of my body, waging war against the law of my mind and making me a prisoner of the law of sin at work within my members. What a wretched man I am! Who will rescue me from this body of death? (Romans 7:21-24)

So, how does one walk by faith and be saved? The Spirit helps us here by bringing the Bible into our lives. *The Bible is the revelation of God and his spiritual world.* The Spirit rarely (in our day) shows us anything apart from the Bible; the two work together to shine the light on us. Jesus said it best.

> Yet a time is coming and has now come when the true worshipers will worship the Father in *Spirit* and *truth*, for they are the kind of worshipers the Father seeks. God is Spirit, and his worshipers must worship in *Spirit* and in *truth*. (John 4:23-24)

The Bible without the Spirit is still truth, but there's no light in our minds and hearts when we read it. We don't understand it; it's foolishness to us. But when the Spirit reveals the world that the Bible is talking about, we suddenly see its glory and we want it.

> We have not received the spirit of the world but the Spirit who is from God, that we may understand what God has

freely given us. This is what we speak, not in words taught us by human wisdom but in words taught by the Spirit, expressing spiritual truths in spiritual words. (1 Corinthians 2:12-13)

We will see in a later chapter what the Spirit wants us to see in the Bible. We want to make the point here, however, that faith is impossible without the Bible. Light comes from it alone.

How, then, can they call on the one they have not believed in? And how can they believe in the one of whom they have not heard? And how can they hear without someone preaching to them? Consequently, faith comes from hearing the message, and the message is heard through the word of Christ. (Romans 10:14, 17)

Faith is what our father Abraham discovered as God was working with him. (Romans 4:1) Faith always starts with the Word of God, because it's a *response* to God when he's talking to us. Abraham started there.

The LORD had said to Abram, "Leave your country, your people and your father's household and go to the land I will show you." (Genesis 12:1)

And when God spoke to him, the Spirit of God brought Abraham into the presence of God so that he could see the One speaking and hear these words as from the mouth of God. He had no doubt about what was happening. He knew it wasn't his imagination; somehow God came into his life and made himself known.

So, we have this definition of faith in Hebrews.

Now faith is being sure of what we hope for and certain of what we do not see. (Hebrews 11:1)

His being sure and certain came from the Holy Spirit's work of revealing God to him apart from physical means (in other words, he believed what he couldn't see with his physical senses). So faith isn't *hoping* that something will happen, it's *knowing* that it will happen, in spite of what your senses are telling you.

Put in another way, *faith is walking in the light of God's world.* The Holy Spirit turns the light on, so to speak, so that we can see the invisible, spiritual world of God.

> I am the light of the world. Whoever follows me will never walk in darkness, but will have the light of life. (John 8:12)

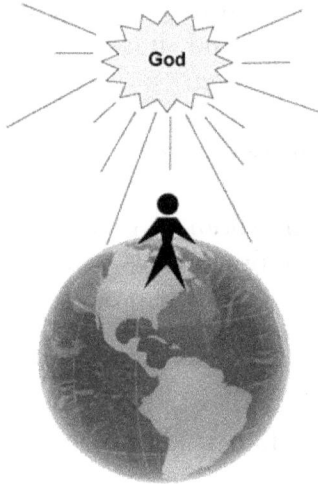

The Spirit of Christ reveals God to us; we see his glory and unique nature, his holiness. He reveals our own hearts and our helplessness and need. He reveals the way to God, through Christ alone. He reveals this world to us and how worthless it is for our spiritual needs. He reveals the treasures of Heaven, the enemy to avoid, and our brothers and sisters in the church. As soon as we are born again into God's Kingdom we start seeing these realities.

Faith, then, is living with those realities. The person who knows what's really going on around him can avoid danger and take the right road to life. He sees things that others can't see, and the quality of his life proves his confession.

What does the Spirit show us in the Bible? What are the kinds of things that we will learn there that will help us survive in dark times and find the way to life and safety? Look for this precious knowledge across the entire Bible, in both the Old and New Testaments.

- *The Kingdom of God* – God is a King, and he rules over his subjects: *us*. If you don't want to run afoul of the political power over you, you will learn his Law, his ways, his Kingdom principles, and obey him in all things. The blessing of this arrangement is that he is sworn to protect, provide for, and make prosperous his people. Here is our refuge and peace and security.

- *Cleansing from sin* – God is holy, and only those who have purified their hearts and minds of all sin and rebellion against him will be allowed into his presence. He extends his pleasure only toward willing, holy subjects; the wicked will be destroyed. And we dare not go by our own definition of what is sin and what is righteousness; God insists that we use his standard – the Law, or Torah, spelled out in the Books of Moses.

- *Creation design* – God made his world to run a certain way. Man, however, in turning away from God, twisted the world to suit his own ends, in ways that would fulfill his lusts. In other words, we've broken the world. Now all through the Bible we find God instructing us about how to use his world in the right way, how to walk in the paths that he laid down for us at Creation. Proverbs is a good start on this kind of information; it tells us how to live at peace with both God and man.

- *The heart of man* – Very few people understand what brought about such chaos and misery in our world. You can tell, because they blame God and whatever other scapegoat they can for their troubles. The trouble, however, is in ourselves. We little know the deep and powerful nature of our own sin. Here is where we have to start, if we want to work our way out of our problems. That is, in fact, where Jesus starts. "He shall save his people from their sins." (Matthew 1:21)

- ***The mercy of God*** – Our long alienation from God has left us with a hole in our understanding of God. It's true, God is a terror to the wicked; the sinner is understandably fearful of appearing before this holy God. But imagine our surprise when we find God willing to take us back and forget the past! Here is an aspect of God that will prove to be a rich treasure, a hope beyond hope that there will be solutions to correct the fatal inclination of our sinful nature. He can and will cure our sinful nature and make us *willing* to walk in righteousness and holiness.

- ***The Judge*** – One reason we keep living in sin is that we think that we can get away with it, that nobody will know about what we're doing or thinking. When we come face to face with God, however, such a lie dissolves like a vapor. Here is someone who knows our very thoughts. Nothing we've done has escaped him. His standards of righteousness are terrifying. "Nothing in all creation is hidden from God's sight. Everything is uncovered and laid bare before the eyes of him to whom we must give account." (Hebrews 4:13) It's a healthy exercise to read the Prophets regularly, because here we face the Judge who knows the whole earth; he expects perfection from all of us, and can easily see that we don't measure up. Here, too, are the sentences of the Judge made plain against the wicked, and the only hope of the righteous.

- ***Victory in Christ*** – We cannot overemphasize the importance of Jesus Christ to God's people. He suffered the worst that this world could throw at him. He suffered under the work of the Enemy. He even suffered under the hand of his own Father, bringing our punishment upon his head and separating him from God at death. He prevailed over it all. Risen from the dead to die no more, he sits at God's right hand reigning with him over all things to eternity. *That's our future, our hope* – to live with Christ. We can't fail, because he won already. Being one with him means that we *already* have the victory over sin and death. It's just a matter of time, suffering under a few "light and momentary troubles" in this world, and then we will put all that behind us forever.

- *The end of all things* – In times of despair, when everything is failing and the world collapsing, when "the wicked get what the righteous deserve and the righteous get what the wicked deserve," we start wondering if the promises of God in the Bible are really true. Is this upside-down world going to win after all? There doesn't seem to be much hope for us here! But the Bible shows us in many places a preview of what's to come. God is going to win in the end. Those who have been faithful unto death will reign with him over a new Heaven and earth. The book of Revelation was designed especially with this in mind: to give hope to the people of God in their darkest hour. The dawn is coming.

In Christianity alone is light. Every other religion and philosophy is in some form of darkness. We alone have the entire picture in our Bible. That may sound like religious arrogance, but we are only basing this statement on God's claim.

> Jesus answered, "I am the way and the truth and the life. No one comes to the Father except through me. If you really knew me, you would know my Father as well. From now on, you do know him and have seen him." (John 14:6-7)

This is not a time for doubt but for faith. If you want to follow someone else's roadmap that leads to disaster, that's up to you; but the wise will listen to the only One who has life, and will follow him.

According to the Covenant requirements, all of Abraham's children are going to live by faith, not by sight, because the promises are fulfilled in Heaven, not on earth.

> If you belong to Christ, then you are Abraham's seed, and heirs according to the promise. (Galatians 3:29)

Love not the world

The second plank in the raft that helps us survive hardships is being able to cut our ties with this world. This too is a skill that is not easily learned or carried out. Our life-training so far has consisted in learning how to get along in this world, the very opposite of what God wants us to do. We have to un-learn our complete dependence on (and love for) this world, and learn how to get along without it.

There are two meanings to the word "world" in the Bible. God made the world, in the beginning, and it was beautiful; his Creation was "very good" in his eyes. That's why John 3:16 says that he so loves the world. In the beginning, God made the world with "wisdom and understanding." (Jeremiah 10:12) This means that every part of his world had its place, its role, its purpose in the overall picture. Every part was specially made to make its contribution to the world around it, and to benefit from all the parts around it. Like a watchmaker who crafts each piece to fit into the whole watch that works with precision, God made the world full of unique parts that collectively made a Paradise.

This of course requires profound wisdom. Scientists are only beginning to plumb the depths of creation, both on a microscopic level as well as the cosmic level. The deeper they investigate, the more they learn that this world is unimaginably complex, yet beautifully fitted together. The mind of man can only stand back in awe over such a work of art that God has made.

But in 1 John the word "world" means what man, and his partner Satan, has turned God's world into – a drunken orgy, so to speak.

> Do not love the world or anything in the world. If anyone loves the world, the love of the Father is not in him. For everything in the world – the cravings of sinful man, the lust of his eyes and the boasting of what he has and does – comes not from the Father but from the world. (1 John 2:15-16)

When man rebelled against God, he died to God; he lost the ability to stay in touch with the mind and wisdom and power of God. He became an enemy of God. That could only spell trouble for creation.

When man lost his connection with God, with raging lusts that demanded to be satisfied, and no options for getting back to God and straightening this situation out, he started a new project: to re-create this world to fulfill his lusts and desires. If he couldn't have God's goodness, then he would create his own. To this day humanity has been fanatically busy creating a world that gives them the satisfactions and thrills and riches and security that they want. We call it "the good life," the American Dream, or Utopia. It's a life of wealth, power, lust and entertainment and, in many cases, vengeance, war and repression. We've replaced what God thought was "good" (Genesis 1:31) with what *we* think is good. But God hates it. It's actually idolatry, because we now worship the objects of our lusts instead of the Creator.

> Put to death, therefore, whatever belongs to your earthly nature: sexual immorality, impurity, lust, evil desires and greed, which is idolatry. (Colossians 3:5)

Man doesn't have God's wisdom. God can create a universe with parts that fit together perfectly. Man, however, creates a disaster. He can't anticipate what will happen when he creates new machines and chemicals and governments and cultures, no matter what good intentions he may have. Notice that there is always a downside to man's works, for two reasons: *first*, God has a curse on this creation, which means he will make sure that we get hurt and frustrated working with it (see the story of Babel). He certainly isn't going to reward us in our rebellion! *Second*, we don't understand the materials we're working with well enough to avoid potential problems; we're always being surprised by hidden flaws.

In other words we have left the goodness of God (remember that he called what *he* made "very good" – Genesis 1:31) and are trying desperately to create another "good" out of the ingredients of this world without God's direction. But there's a problem in that: this world wasn't designed to fulfill the heart and life of man; only God can do that.

The world works in ways that God despises. It loves numbers, power, winning, destruction and slaughter, oppression, wealth, influence, reputation, politicking, lies and deceit, hatred, and living for pleasure. This is the way it solves its problems and satisfies its lusts. We've recreated God's perfect paradise into a playground for our lusts, passions, murders, greed, robberies, insurrection, etc. The new world "system," we could call it. It is a world full of temptation, where the opportunities for immorality abound. It's like a circus where people wander from sideshow to sideshow, tasting this forbidden sweet, trying that immoral practice – all set up for our pleasure. People who live like this have nothing to do with God, nor do they understand him.

This new world that we've been creating has been programmed into our hearts and brains since birth. We were raised in it; we've been taught to respect its rules, we value its treasures, we suffer under its shortcomings – it's literally the only world that we know. Just becoming a Christian doesn't take all of that out of our hearts overnight!

> As for you, you were dead in your transgressions and sins, in which you used to live when you followed the ways of this world and of the ruler of the kingdom of the air, the spirit who is now at work in those who are disobedient. All of us also lived among them at one time, gratifying the cravings of our sinful nature and following its desires and thoughts. Like the rest, we were by nature objects of wrath. (Ephesians 2:1-3)

If we think that we leave the world behind us at the church door, we are foolish. Each of us has been programmed by the world system since the day we were born. We church-goers still think the way the world taught us to think; our whole being still responds strongly to the world's ways and temptations. Each of us, as the saying goes, brings a lot of baggage with us into the church – baggage that interferes with our Mission.

As we learn about the new world of God that we've been made a part of in Christ, we also have to put the old world aside. It's going to get in the way of everything we do. In fact, it's so deeply ingrained in us that we will be surprised how quickly we go back to our old ways.

> You were taught, with regard to your former way of life, to put off your old self, which is being corrupted by its deceitful desires; to be made new in the attitude of your minds; and to put on the new self, created to be like God in true righteousness and holiness. (Ephesians 4:22-24)

The kind of life that we want to live now is one where God rules, not man. We want the treasures of Heaven, not the treasures of this world. We want God's approval, not man's. We love righteousness, not wickedness. We wage war against God's enemies, not our neighbor, with weapons forged in Heaven, not earth's weapons. We live by the Spirit, not the flesh, and we strive to be filled with the fruit of the Spirit in our lives, not with what fulfills the desires of the sinful nature.

We have done things our way for so long that it's going to be a long, tedious training period to cut our ties with this world and forge new ones with God's world. Most people just can't leave this world behind; like Lot's wife, they love this world and its ways too much to exchange it for a spiritual world they can't see. What they don't realize is that *God* is going to take everything away from them. He's going to force people into a dilemma: either walk on water, or drown. He's certainly not going to wait for us to train ourselves! He deliberately throws us into the deep end, so to speak, and forces us to learn how to swim. It's time to learn how to cut our ties with this world.

True Christians will survive in times of trouble, times when they lose everything in this world, because they're standing on a spiritual foundation. Like the saints of the Bible, they care little if what they have in this world is taken from them. They've learned how to live with spiritual treasures.

> For he was looking forward to the city with foundations,
> whose architect and builder is God. (Hebrews 11:10)

We're going to need some help in this area. We're not used to letting go of our world. It hurts to give it up; it induces panic, because we think we can't live without certain "essentials" of life. Yet Jesus keeps pushing us to do that very thing, as if he sees something that we don't see.

> He said to another man, "Follow me." But the man replied, "Lord, first let me go and bury my father." Jesus said to him, "Let the dead bury their own dead, but you go and proclaim the kingdom of God."

Still another said, "I will follow you, Lord; but first let me go back and say good-by to my family." Jesus replied, "No one who puts his hand to the plow and looks back is fit for service in the kingdom of God." (Luke 9:59-62)

Do not be afraid, little flock, for your Father has been pleased to give you the kingdom. Sell your possessions and give to the poor. Provide purses for yourselves that will not wear out, a treasure in Heaven that will not be exhausted, where no thief comes near and no moth destroys. For where your treasure is, there your heart will be also. (Luke 12:32)

Jesus answered, "If you want to be perfect, go, sell your possessions and give to the poor, and you will have treasure in Heaven. Then come, follow me." When the young man heard this, he went away sad, because he had great wealth. Then Jesus said to his disciples, "I tell you the truth, it is hard for a rich man to enter the kingdom of Heaven. Again I tell you, it is easier for a camel to go through the eye of a needle than for a rich man to enter the kingdom of God." (Matthew 19:21-24)

Jesus didn't hesitate to put his finger on some very sensitive issues with us. For example, he knows that many of us will put even our physical families ahead of God. This is a serious mistake in God's eyes. Your family will rarely be supportive in your walk of faith; they will more often be a hindrance to you. The time will come when you will have to choose between them and God; you can't have both.

Do not suppose that I have come to bring peace to the earth. I did not come to bring peace, but a sword. For I have come to turn "a man against his father, a daughter against her mother, a daughter-in-law against her mother-in-law – a man's enemies will be the members of his own household."
Anyone who loves his father or mother more than me is not worthy of me; anyone who loves his son or daughter more than me is not worthy of me; and anyone who does not take his cross and follow me is not worthy of me. (Matthew 10:34-38)

Even our physical well-being will be a target for hardship and trial, and we have to be willing to suffer in our bodies for God's sake. This also requires faith: we have to be able to see what's really going on in our suffering. Jesus, again, provides insight to help us here.

> Blessed are you when people insult you, persecute you and falsely say all kinds of evil against you because of me. Rejoice and be glad, because great is your reward in Heaven, for in the same way they persecuted the prophets who were before you. (Matthew 5:11-12)

Paul, too, had the faith to understand and accept the cross of physical suffering. He knew that, in God's hands (no matter what the immediate cause!), it was designed to strengthen his faith in Christ and grow him spiritually.

> There was given me a thorn in my flesh, a messenger of Satan, to torment me. Three times I pleaded with the Lord to take it away from me. But he said to me, "My grace is sufficient for you, for my power is made perfect in weakness." Therefore I will boast all the more gladly about my weaknesses, so that Christ's power may rest on me. That is why, for Christ's sake, I delight in weaknesses, in insults, in hardships, in persecutions, in difficulties. For when I am weak, then I am strong. (2 Corinthians 12:7-10)

All these are aspects about the deceitfulness and danger of this world. The wise Christian is going to be wary about these things from now on. The only world that we can depend on completely is God's new Kingdom. Our only hope and true delight is going to be the new world in Heaven. Our only family who cares for us spiritually is the Church. In this world we are only passing through, trying to avoid the pitfalls and dangers as we make our way to Heaven.

> All these people were still living by faith when they died. They did not receive the things promised; they only saw them and welcomed them from a distance. And they admitted that they were aliens and strangers on earth. People who say such things show that they are looking for a country of their own.

If they had been thinking of the country they had left, they would have had opportunity to return. Instead, they were longing for a better country – a Heavenly one. Therefore God is not ashamed to be called their God, for he has prepared a city for them. (Hebrews 11:13-16)

That means, then, that in order to survive we have to have a "light touch" on the things of this world. We aren't suggesting that you go out and "sell everything you have and give it to the poor." It's true, there are some people who need to do that, and Jesus will expect it of them when the time comes; it's his privilege to decide that. For most of us, however, we are called to work and provide for our families and have some extra resources on hand to help others in the church. A normal life, in other words – not greed, not piling up treasures in this world, but being thankful for what God gives you and blesses you with.

The time will come, however, when one or more of those blessings is going to be threatened. That will be the test of your spiritual character. How willing will you be to let it go?

"Naked I came from my mother's womb, and naked I will depart. The LORD gave and the LORD has taken away; may the name of the LORD be praised." In all this, Job did not sin by charging God with wrongdoing. (Job 1:21-22)

Many Christians would have great difficulty giving up what they think they can't live without – like food, shelter, good health, and safety, for themselves and their loved ones. Yet in times of great suffering on a widespread scale in society, this is exactly what they will be called to do. It will require a deep-rooted faith, and a light touch indeed on the things of this world, to be able to say with Paul –

I know what it is to be in need, and I know what it is to have plenty. I have learned the secret of being content in any and every situation, whether well fed or hungry, whether living in plenty or in want. I can do everything through him who gives me strength. (Philippians 4:12-13)

Consider the alternative! What if God relented and didn't put you through any hard times or suffering? What would happen to you? You would do no better than the Israelites who, in their new ease and prosperity, forgot God. They were so taken up with life in this world that they had no interest, no perceived need, for anything in God's world. Physical pleasures and security deaden our spirits and make us forget about God, and our spiritual standing with him. That's sinful human nature at work. We are *all* like that. But what will you do in the end? The world is going down; do you want to go down with it? Isn't it a mercy, then, when God "reminds" you, even with harsh discipline, that your home is not here?

God loves his people, and that's why he puts hardships in their lives. It brings in the necessary discipline that they will need to wean them from a disappointing, shallow world and seek the deep, deep love of God in Christ. They get a military mindset about this world, when they are forced to fight against it and suffer in it. The Lord left enemies in the Promised Land for this very reason.

> These are the nations the LORD left to test all those Israelites who had not experienced any of the wars in Canaan (he did this only to **teach warfare** to the descendants of the Israelites who had not had previous battle experience). (Judges 3:1-2)

So, by God's design we are going to have hard times to suffer through. It's part of our spiritual growth process.

> And you have forgotten that word of encouragement that addresses you as sons: "My son, do not make light of the Lord's discipline, and do not lose heart when he rebukes you, because the Lord disciplines those he loves, and he punishes everyone he accepts as a son."
> Endure hardship as discipline; God is treating you as sons. For what son is not disciplined by his father? If you are not disciplined (and everyone undergoes discipline), then you are illegitimate children and not true sons. Moreover, we have all had human fathers who disciplined us and we respected them for it. How much more should we submit to

the Father of our spirits and live! Our fathers disciplined us for a little while as they thought best; but God disciplines us for our good, that we may share in his holiness. No discipline seems pleasant at the time, but painful. Later on, however, it produces a harvest of righteousness and peace for those who have been trained by it. (Hebrews 12:5-11)

God has his reasons for taking away our physical blessings; we dare not accuse him of mistreating us. Unknown to us, this physical blessing may be taking our hearts away from God. Denying it to us may be a mercy, not a curse; it may be our salvation.

Or, as in Job's case, it may simply be a matter of God proving our faith to doubters like the devil. He apparently had no reason for allowing Job to suffer other than to show what faith can do for us in times of trial.

Have you considered my servant Job? There is no one on earth like him; he is blameless and upright, a man who fears God and shuns evil. (Job 1:8)

What an honor to be a showcase of God's mercy and grace holding up a poor creature like me, so that I might be to his praise and glory! Others will see the power and wisdom of God in me as *I trust in him alone*, something that the people of this world can't bring themselves to do – even though it's our only hope of survival.

Always be prepared to give an answer to everyone who asks you to give the reason for the hope that you have. But do this with gentleness and respect, keeping a clear conscience, so that those who speak maliciously against your good behavior in Christ may be ashamed of their slander. (1 Peter 3:15-16)

The survivor's secret

So, the point in being a survivor is twofold:

- *First*, you must learn to walk with God. God is Spirit, and his world is spiritual. Your calling is to live with God in

Heaven someday. To do that, you must learn what God is like, you must learn his ways, you must set your heart on "things above," you must learn to *love* God. These aren't going to be easy things to learn. We are so physical, so tied down to this physical world of ours, that it's going to take a great deal of training to live with God. While others sink beneath the waves of the storm, Christians, like Peter, will feel the hands of Christ holding them on top of the waves. The storm doesn't go away, but God's people survive through it because they rest in him.

The beauty and power of this kind of life show up during hard times. When other people are distressed, in confusion and in despair, the Christian lives in peace and security. Nothing shakes his hope and confidence in God. He also will probably suffer loss, but he passes off the loss as a small thing. He lives and feeds off the Bread of Life, and his life of faith shows it. The martyrs of history were wonderful examples of this joyful, quiet confidence in their God and his support when they were led to the stake. They were already living in another world. That ability didn't come to them overnight!

- *Second*, you must begin cutting your ties to sin and this world. Jesus called it "crucifying yourselves." Now crucifixion is *not* pleasant! It's painful, it's confusing, and we would do anything else rather than go through with it. But it's necessary for our spiritual development. We can't enter Heaven, we won't enjoy the treasures of Heaven, if our hearts are like Lot's wife: she couldn't tear herself away from the "good" life here, so she wasn't allowed into the next life with God.

Having cut your ties with sin and the world has another powerful aspect to it during hard times. It helps you survive spiritually when those physical blessings are forcibly taken away from you. It gives you strength by depending on God alone when you have to go without even the necessities of life. Paul "learned the secret of being content in any and every situation, whether well fed or hungry, whether living in plenty or in want." (Philippians 4:12) If he hadn't learned this secret, he would never have made it. Many others failed under similar loads while Paul the survivor was still struggling on. In fact, the loss of health and wealth is probably the best way to reveal where our hearts really are – in this world or the next. That's one reason why God lets his people go through hard times.

Personal Holiness

Holiness is not just "being good." There's a lot of confusion about what holiness is, because most people think that holiness is the same thing as righteousness. Actually it has a much deeper, more profound meaning than "being good."

Righteousness is being good. Righteousness is defined by the Law of God (the *Torah*), which is the set of Laws that we have in the first five books of the Bible. There are 613 laws in the Torah. The Ten Commandments are a summary of those 613 laws, and the two greatest commandments (Matthew 22:36-40) are a summary of the Ten. The Law describes the kind of life that God wants to see us live. If we live like the Law describes, then we will be allowed into his presence. If we don't conform to the Law – in other words, if we are rebels and lawless and refuse to have God rule over us – then of course he wants nothing to do with us.

> And if we are careful to obey all this Law before the LORD our God, as he has commanded us, that will be our righteousness. (Deuteronomy 6:25)

Righteousness is part of the holy life, but it's not all of it. Holiness is a bigger concept than just righteousness. Holiness deals with actually living with God, once we get the right to enter into his presence. Righteousness gets us into the Holy of Holies, and *holiness is the new way of life* that we will have with God in that Holy of Holies.

A God-centered life

We have been so self-centered for all our lives that it's hard to fathom the idea of taking God so seriously. The whole universe revolves around us, it seems; our interests focus on how *we* feel and what *we* want.

43

Perhaps the closest we get to understanding how someone else can be the focus of our lives is when we fall in love with someone. Then we aren't thinking of ourselves at all; the way the other person moves, the way they talk, everything about them fascinates us and holds us captive in a helpless wonder.

We were designed to love God in this way. Man was originally given the ability to know God; he had the spiritual awareness of the presence of God. Adam lived in two worlds at the same time: in this physical world, and also in God's spiritual world. He had to be able to do this, because his responsibilities included getting orders direct from God for ruling over the earth according to God's will. Everything depended on Adam loving what he saw in God; otherwise he wouldn't be inclined to carry out *God's* will on earth.

In fact, Adam's soul found its chief joy in God, because *God is the source of all good things*. Adam would have delighted to bring God to every situation, and showing off the beauty and wisdom and power and excellence of God. God would have an enthusiastic partner in his program to display his glory in all the world.

Unfortunately man unplugged himself from God, like a light bulb from its power, and the enthusiasm left. He lives his life here in darkness. He can't see God nor can he know him. He fears this God who holds the Law over his guilty soul; he refuses to come to God for help. Instead of loving God (and that requires at least the ability to know God, which we can't in our rebellion!), mankind hates God because he keeps interfering with our personal program of creating a playground for our lusts in this broken creation.

Fortunately the story doesn't end there. In Christ, there are a few who are restored to fellowship with God. Christians, brought to life spiritually by the Word and the Spirit, know God, just as Adam was made to do. The idea is to bring man back to God: not only to Adam's level of knowledge, but even deeper into the Temple. Now the children of God have the privilege of knowing God *as Jesus the Son knows him*.

Need drives us to God. We really have to be convinced that there's no hope anywhere else, before we turn to God with all of our hearts. Our tendency is to try anything else but him; we are so unfamiliar with him and his world that we think our best bet is to look to this world's wisdom, wealth and power first. We have lived this way all of our lives. But when nothing is working, God calls yet again and draws us to himself, to discover a new world that has real answers. What a revelation! No wonder the Bible counsels us to "Taste and see that the LORD is good; blessed is the man who takes refuge in him." (Psalm 34:8)

> Blessed are those you choose and bring near to live in your courts! We are filled with the good things of your house, of your holy temple. (Psalm 65:4)

The closer we get to him, the more we realize what we've been missing out on. Here is the solution to all of our problems! What we needed all along was to come to the throne of God and request what he has for us – his spiritual treasures. His wisdom enlightens the most obscure darkness; his power untangles the most complex problem; his love overcomes the most terrible loneliness. He corrects our wrong notions, he rebukes us for our sin without hesitation, and he leads us in the way of life. God blesses us with what our souls need: peace, joy, righteousness, perseverance, courage, faith.

The more time we spend in God's presence, the more we appreciate what he is, and the more we depend on him for not only daily needs but help in times of disaster. Take some time out and compare what life used to be like without God against what it is like with him. It's like night and day. God gives what this world can *never* give. That taste of power and joy from Heaven is what keeps the child of God coming back to God in his time of need. He becomes God-centered now; he looks forward to experiencing the presence of God again and again. Somehow, going back to the world is such a let-down!

> How lovely is your dwelling place, O LORD Almighty! My soul yearns, even faints, for the courts of the LORD; my heart and my flesh cry out for the living God. (Psalm 84:1-2)

If you wonder just how much God will bless you with, whether he holds anything back from you, consider this: when you first believed in Jesus as your Savior from sin and death, God made you *one with Christ*. Our union with the Son of God puts us in an amazing position.

Now we can know God as Jesus knows him. Nobody is closer to the Father than his own Son; the Father withholds nothing from his Son. In that position, we too will know and experience God without limit, without reservation.

> All that belongs to the Father is mine. That is why I said the Spirit will take from what is mine and make it known to you. (John 16:15)

Though all this is waiting for us in Heaven, we can taste the "first-fruits" of this special relationship now, in this world. In fact, this is what helps us survive in a world filled with the very opposite of joy and peace and righteousness. Our secret life with God, in Christ, will keep us going when everything around us falls apart. This is the secret to spiritual survival – to *walk with God.*

So, the *holy life* means living with this God and enjoying him. It's more than being good; it's getting in touch with God and having him change us, fill us, guide us, protect us, and enrich us as we make our way to Heaven. We are being changed into his image, spiritually. Holiness is being God-centered; we draw on him in the same way that we do our food and water and air. He is, literally, our life. Nothing in this world, no matter how bad it gets, can touch this new life in us.

This is a survival skill that few "Christians" have. Most people play at religion: reciting creeds and singing hymns and listening to sermons, as if these activities in themselves make them "holy." They would be startled, perhaps fearful, at encountering God anywhere along the way. It never seems to occur to them that the point of these religious exercises is to come into God's presence and touch *him.* Then when troubles come, they find out that their "religion" doesn't do them any good. They are just as much without answers, and just as helpless in the hands of the enemy, as any unbeliever would be.

How can we tell, then, that we are walking with God? What is the Christian doing that keeps that relationship alive between him and God? He certainly isn't waiting until disaster happens to work on it! Just as a living body has some vital signs that prove the presence of life, the true Christian who is centered on God will show certain spiritual signs of life. These things prove that this person really is in touch with God. When you see these four vital signs, be encouraged: it means that this person is going to make it spiritually.

First vital sign – Prayer

Almost everyone prays at some point or another. Problems drive us to God; we know that he can do things that we can't do, so we show up on his doorstep pleading for help. Very few people get answers to their prayers, however, from the God of the Bible. He actually ignores most prayers, because he looks at the heart, not at the problem. Often (is this surprising to you?) he usually doesn't like what he sees there.

It's not as if he can't help you – he can fix anything! But when people have the wrong attitude toward God, that bothers him more than their problems do. The Bible plainly warns us that pride, the lack of faith, self-centeredness, or a heart fixed on things of this world, will only result in silence from Heaven.

If you pray as if God owes you something, you'll never get anywhere with him. He doesn't owe anybody anything! He also doesn't agree to any deals that people try to make with him. We have sinned away any "rights" that we may try to claim from him. From now on, anything he gives us will be out of mercy – an undeserved gift.

When people ask for the wrong things, instead of focusing on what he knows that they need, such prayers fail to move him. Why would he give you gold when he has spiritual treasures to hand out? Why would he give you physical safety when the Cross is the very doorway to life with him? Why do you close your eyes to God's true riches and insist that he give you the empty, worthless shadows of this world? God's spiritual world is going to last forever! Why focus on this passing world of ours that is scheduled to be destroyed soon?

You will find, if God is merciful to you and teaches you how to pray, that true prayer that gets answers will reach out for *him*, not this world. The answers that we need come from Heaven, not from earth. We focus on things above, not things below. We are in training to live with him in Heaven, a spiritual world. So let's leave Sodom behind, as Lot did.

True prayer is a humbling experience. Our God is so good to us, though we don't deserve anything from him. God knows far better what we need from him than we do. God is running the universe – which means he doesn't need our help or opinions; he'll give us what we need when we need it, according to his own schedule. God's main concern is fixing the damage that our sin has caused. To him, that issue comes first, even before health and wealth and security. We may barge into the throne room of Heaven with a long list of "prayer requests" for his immediate attention; but if we could see him in faith, there in his glory, all of our childish notions would look so foolish in light of the great concerns of the Throne of God. We may as well tear up our list and start a new one; it's time to find out what *he* wants for us.

The first step of prayer, then, is to quiet ourselves before his throne. It is time to submit ourselves to him, not tell him what to do or demand anything. Faith will show us that here is a power and wisdom beyond our understanding. It is time to report to him as an "unworthy servant," not as a demanding child.

The second step is to listen and learn. We come to him because we have terrible problems, but we don't understand the situation as he does. He knows "the end from the beginning." He knows the people and places and times that are involved, and we know hardly anything about it. All we know is our own little part in the picture. It seems that we can't bear to suffer like this anymore, but in God's presence we learn that this trial is our medicine, the healing process to change us from sinner to saint. Would we really have him stop the healing process? You see, prayer is not telling God what to do; prayer is learning about what God is doing. Prayer enlightens us; it encourages us to persevere; it strengthens us to follow his will; it corrects us in our wayward thoughts and actions. If you need help in this aspect of prayer, study Jesus' prayer in the Garden of Gethsemane (see Matthew 26:36-44).

There's a popular saying going around that says "prayer changes things." I understand what it's trying to say, but I think that a more appropriate thing to say is this: Prayer changes *you*. Prayer isn't supposed to be demanding something from God: "God, you have to give me what I want!" Prayer is submitting yourself to God to do what *he* wants. We pray about our troubles, about a difficult situation, about our needs – but the proper attitude is to bring these needs to the Throne of Grace and be ready for whatever God has for you in response. Don't be surprised if it isn't what you were expecting from him!

> In the middle of *difficult trials* – he will give you faith and strength to last through them.

> In the middle of *great loss* – he will give you himself as a replacement.

> In the middle of *loneliness* – he will teach you to walk with him.

> In the middle of *social upheaval* – he will teach you how to be a spiritual blessing and strength to others.

You see, God has a different agenda than we have. Never go to God demanding a certain answer from him. You don't know the situation as he does. You may not have realized that he set up this problem of yours to *drive* you to him. He has new spiritual resources waiting for you to come and claim from him, and learn how to use. Prayer is going to be an enlightening experience for you, a learning experience. You will find a spiritual God that you can stand on, a foundation that is not of this world, a rock that will hold you up when you lose everything else in this world that you used to depend on so much, things that you thought you couldn't do without. Prayer is opening up the doors to Heaven to lay hold of the spiritual treasures that Jesus told us about. Prayer is the first step in training ourselves to turn to God, and trust in him alone for all of our needs. It's the discovery that we need God, not this world.

> Do not be afraid, Abram. I am your shield, your very great reward. (Genesis 15:1)

Of course, this would become more obvious to us if we spent more time in his Word. Prayer would be less of a disappointment to us and more of a training session if we prayed intelligently, not ignorantly. God has an agenda for us; his plan is to save us and bring us to himself in Heaven to live with him. There is much to be done to accomplish all this. The Bible tells us what God wants to give us that will enable us to reach those goals. For example, the Bible tells us that God is the King, and that Jesus is building a Kingdom here on earth among us, and that we are his subjects who are obligated to serve him. So, prayer is a matter of us showing up at the throne and submitting ourselves to *his will*. "Lord, teach me your will! And give me the will to follow it with all my heart."

This is what makes the Bible so important for prayer. We learn what to ask for. God has certain treasures and resources ready for his people, in the middle of all their needs; all he wants is for us to recognize those treasures and ask for them. God already knows how to fix this broken world; he wants us to learn his will and fall in line with his will so that we can work *with* him instead of against him. All of this information is in the Bible, though it takes a great deal of learning, meditation, determination, and spiritual growth to ask for *that* when we pray. But a spiritually mature Christian wouldn't dare ask for anything else!

Once we get the right attitude when we approach God, and we learn what to pray for, the last thing we have to master in prayer is knowing how to *wait on him*. God has his own schedule and set of priorities. He doesn't always give us what we ask for, even if we do need it. There are many reasons for this: *first*, you may not be ready for it yet. You may have to learn a few things first, or get rid of some sin, before he can give you something that you would need spiritual maturity to handle. *Second*, there are a lot of other people and circumstances involved besides yourself, and you may have to wait until the time is ripe. *Third*, God will often hold back from giving you something because he wants to see if you *really* want it. What you really need is a spiritual treasure to solve your problem; but what will you do if you don't get it right away? Will you go back to the world and try something else, or is God's answer the only option for you, so much so that you will wait no matter how long it takes? "Though he slay me, yet will I hope in him." (Job 13:15) You can tell if you have faith – the ability to see the true wealth in God's resources – if you never give up waiting for God's answers.

So, a spiritual survivor will pray to survive *spiritually*. He asks for treasures from Heaven, because he knows how empty this world's treasures are. He prays for faith, for perseverance to seek God, for strength to withstand storms with his heart and his hope set on the Rock. He wants to come through this storm *alive and well in Christ*, not having fallen away from him. In other words, the hardship becomes an opportunity to test yourself, to strengthen yourself: are you able and willing to throw yourself completely on God and not worry about your standing in this world?

Crucifying sin

Sin is man's biggest problem. Everything he does is tainted with it. It's an attitude, a rebellious spirit, that makes him turn away from God and live without him. Sin is a deliberate rejection of the rule of God over his life. Even the nicest people are going to reject God's Law in some way, because we are all born sinners.

Yet most Christians put away the subject of sin as soon as they are converted. They got forgiveness for their sin through Christ, and they know that the Father accepts them now in Christ, as if that sin was put away from them "as far as the east is from the west." Conversion, however, did not get rid of our old nature. It was a transaction between us and God that made it possible for us to know him, come to him, and live with him. It was the first legal step that we had to take in order to enter Heaven.

The *second* step, however, is just as important. Now that we are reconciled with God and are at peace with him, we can get down to business and get rid of this sin that fills our hearts and minds. This is the process called *sanctification* – where the Holy Spirit regenerates our hearts and conforms us into the image of Christ, so that we will be fit to live with the holy God. Sanctification is a life-long process.

Many Christians are unaware of how much has to be done in this area. When they go to church, they dress up and look good, they feel good sitting there in the pew, and so they think they *are* good. Little do they know about the simmering spiritual junk that is hiding beneath that religious appearance!

Since God is determined to make us as righteous as his son Jesus, he will often resort to trials and hardships to purify us. Even Jesus "learned obedience" from his Father through trials. He himself had no sins to correct; but the way of righteousness in this fallen world is the way of the cross, not the way of ease and security.

> During the days of Jesus' life on earth, he offered up prayers and petitions with loud cries and tears to the one who could save him from death, and he was heard because of his reverent submission. Although he was a son, he learned obedience from what he suffered and, once made perfect, he became the source of eternal salvation for all who obey him. (Hebrews 5:7-9)

The lesson here is that God will not hesitate to hurt us when we need discipline. Perhaps adults can't connect their trials with the idea of discipline. We know what it was like to be punished by our parents when we were young, but we fail to recognize another "rod of discipline" in the hard circumstances of life. We are, for some reason, very reluctant to admit that God would be doing this to us. *First*, we usually don't think we deserve punishment (will we never grow up?), and *second*, we can't imagine why the God of love would strike us in anger.

God doesn't owe us anything. We don't deserve anything good from him. If we could see but a part of the truth, we would be amazed that he has let us live this long on his earth! We have sinned away any good treatment that he might have been obligated to show us. We have heaped the treasures of this world around us; in our fear and greed we have ignored his spiritual treasures. To make the insult worse, we expect God to keep the physical blessings coming – as if he's duty-bound to shower us with worldly treasures to fulfill our physical lusts!

The truth of the matter is that we are living in God's world on borrowed time. He's only giving us more time so that we will perhaps think about the one thing needful.

> He is patient with you, not wanting anyone to perish,
> but everyone to come to repentance. (2 Peter 3:9)

But if we insist on materialism, living for this world, using God as a servant to provide for our lusts, yet continuing in our sin and rebellion against him, we can expect nothing from God except his overwhelming wrath against such hardened sinners.

> If we deliberately keep on sinning after we have received the knowledge of the truth, no sacrifice for sins is left, but only a fearful expectation of judgment and of raging fire that will consume the enemies of God. (Hebrews 10:26-27)

But he doesn't have wrath against his own children – he has another form of fire. It's going to hurt, we are going to be miserable under Christ's cross, but it's designed to burn the dross from our hearts and minds and force us into Christ's image (since we rarely will do it the easy way). It's a blast furnace of affliction.

The furnace of affliction

Steel makers put the iron ore in a furnace, then heat it until the iron melts out from the rock and slag so that they can pour it off into molds. The junk – or slag – which comes floating to the top of the molten iron is then easily scraped off the top and thrown away. In the same way, God puts the fire of affliction under our lives and refines us, separating the sins and rebellion out of our hearts and minds, so that the only thing left is the pure righteousness of Christ and the fruit of the Holy Spirit.

> For you, O God, tested us; you refined us like silver.
> You brought us into prison and laid burdens on our backs.
> You let men ride over our heads; we went through fire and

water, but you brought us to a place of abundance. (Psalm
66:10-12)

Consider it pure joy, my brothers, whenever you face
trials of many kinds, because you know that the testing of
your faith develops perseverance. Perseverance must finish
its work so that you may be mature and complete, not
lacking anything. (James 1:2-4)

In this you greatly rejoice, though now for a little while
you may have had to suffer grief in all kinds of trials.
These have come so that your faith – of greater worth than
gold, which perishes even though refined by fire – may be
proved genuine and may result in praise, glory and honor
when Jesus Christ is revealed. (1 Peter 1:6-7)

The point is that it hurts – we suffer – under God's rod of
discipline. There are times when he has to switch methods: he changes
from being gentle and easy, to being harsh and tough. Some of us will
only learn this way.

When affliction and trials come, it's time to take stock of our
spiritual standing. If God has resorted to using discipline to get your
attention, you have probably been ignoring him. When life is
comfortable, we tend to ignore God and put spiritual issues on the back
burner.

Otherwise, when you eat and are satisfied, when you
build fine houses and settle down, and when your herds and
flocks grow large and your silver and gold increase and all
you have is multiplied, then your heart will become proud
and you will forget the LORD your God, who brought you
out of Egypt, out of the land of slavery. (Deuteronomy
8:12-14)

We forget that the blessings of the world are actually side-issues to
God. He will take them away from us if need be. If we've become too
caught up with the blessings of this world, perhaps it's time for God to

remove them – one by one, or all at once – and leave us, like Job, sitting destitute in the dust, wondering what in the world happened!

Perhaps, when the Lord was telling you to focus on him, to make him your chief delight, to love him with all your heart, mind and strength, you ignored the warning and looked to other things for joy and comfort. Not that you actually *rejected* God, but you just didn't get around to taking him as seriously as the Word commanded you to. When you prioritized your day, other things took up your time; you left God only a few minutes here and there, a stray thought when you had the extra time. Whether you know it or not, that's an insult to God; you need him more than you think! He deserves more glory and praise than you can imagine. God continually cares for you – he gives you breath and strength to live and work in his world. Does he figure so little in your life that all you can manage is a nod in his direction once in a while? You will find the Lord reacting in anger and destroying the comfortable nest you've built around yourself, and standing you up before him to be dealt with, now, in his way, in a way that will honor him.

Perhaps you have some character issues to work on. Most of us aren't alarmed at all about the spiritual state of our hearts. We knew that Jesus saves us from our sins, and we wanted him to do that; but practically speaking, we have put that crisis behind us now and we're busy going on with life. Little do we know the state of our hearts! God knows – he "judges the thoughts and attitudes of the heart." (Hebrews 4:12) None of us measures up to the perfection of Christ yet. We have the tendency to wreck ourselves and others if left without supervision. We are by no means ready to step into a holy Heaven to live with God. But until we see this, will we take time out to work on this most important of all tasks? Not until we're forced to!

So, God sends afflictions into our lives. Suddenly, as he puts the fire under us, we see all sorts of spiritual junk floating to the top of our character (for everyone to see!) that we didn't know was there: anger, greed, adultery, fear, jealousy, murderous thoughts, pride, rebellion against God, self-will, gluttony, impatience, even idolatry. What a revelation! We've been hiding these sins, these godless acts that we're still so capable of, under the veneer of a comfortable and religious life.

Remove our comforts, and we suddenly become the old sinners that we thought we put behind us.

Affliction brings out our true selves. It is, again, an opportunity to see the truth about ourselves and start the difficult but necessary job of sanctifying our hearts, crucifying our flesh, so that we might be truly holy. Without the affliction we wouldn't have known the truth, nor would we want to know; after it, if we learned our lesson, we will get rid of our sin and grow in righteousness.

So, when you go through hardships, the last thing that God wants to hear from you is whining and crying like a baby. That's what most people do when they have to go through trials. Your duty is to humble yourself before the throne of God and listen to his Word – all of it, wherever the Spirit takes you. After all, if God wanted to give you health and wealth, he could do it in an instant. If he doesn't, then there must be another issue here that you need to examine – you can be sure that it's not God who has the problem! This problem will turn out to your benefit if you have the right attitude: humility under God's discipline, examination of your heart with the Word, confession of whatever sin is in you (no scapegoats or excuses!), and repentance and turning away from that sin. Just be aware that the first time may not be enough. We have a way of "confessing" our sin and then we expect God to stop whipping us immediately. He, however, knows how much discipline it will take to drive it out of our hearts.

> Do not withhold discipline from a child; if you punish
> him with the rod, he will not die. Punish him with the rod
> and save his soul from death. (Proverbs 23:13-14)

This is what makes the difference between spiritual survivors and those who collapse under the weight of hardships. Christians who accept God's heavy hand of discipline are learning from it, changing from it, and accepting it willingly as from a loving Father.

> And we know that in all things God works for the good
> of those who love him, who have been called according to
> his purpose. (Romans 8:28)

Strangely, they are like roses planted in the desert. The hotter it gets, the drier they get, *the more they grow*. They are feeding on the bread of Heaven; the hardships of this world are driving them to God's resources.

So, the spiritual survivor keeps a clear head about him. He knows that sin is the fundamental problem of mankind. *Everything* that God does with man is centered around this issue: he's either going to destroy us over our sin, or fix us. God is not concerned with how comfortable or happy we are; he is concerned about our rebellious attitude toward him. The good times are for later, for Heaven, *after* we take care of this problem of our sin. Those he saves, he changes – first their attitude, then their hearts. The true Christian realizes that *everything* that happens to him is from God's hand for the purpose of *saving him from his sin*. Whatever the cost, whatever the pain involved, we know that God loves us and is purging us from our sin. Always keep that in mind, and you will have a clearer idea of what is happening to you, why it's happening, and where God is taking you with it.

Centered on the Word

We will have a lot to say about doing Bible study in the next chapter, but here we want to look at how important the Bible is to the child of God.

The Bible is quite literally the survivor's manual for the Christian. There's no such thing as survival when your Bible is sitting on the shelf collecting dust. Why in the world people think that they will make it through hard times when they can't even find the Prophets is beyond me!

When we are first converted, we start out with almost no knowledge of God. But one thing in our favor is that God gives us his Spirit, who immediately starts steering us toward life and away from the ways of death. The Spirit will always tug you in the direction of the Bible, because the ways of life are outlined there for us. If we don't follow his lead, we are going to suffer needlessly when hard times come.

The Bible claims to be God's Word.[1] This means, at the simplest level, that ***God spoke these words*** through man. It is not a production of brilliant religious Jews, but a work in spite of them. They would not have known these truths if God had not told them. *God* has spoken; the Bible comes from outside the world; it is *revelation*.

Second, since the Bible is the Word of God, then it is ***authoritative***. If God really wrote this book, then we *must* listen to it – we ignore it at our peril. Our God, not just another human, is speaking to us! These are issues that only God can address; we won't find them explained anywhere else. They pertain to the welfare of our souls, and our relationship with the Creator and King of the universe. We will one day have to give an account to him for what we've heard from the Bible.

Third, since the Bible is the Word of God, then it is the ***truth***. God by definition would have the best and only true insight into the world, even of the mind of man. The Bible is the standard by which all other "truths" are judged. If there is ever a conflict between God's truth and man's truth, then man's "truth" is suspect; God is never wrong, inaccurate, or insufficient for our needs.

These three points force us to take a serious look at the Bible's claims. Because the Bible really is the Word of God, then we cannot ignore it. We must begin studying it and finding out what God has to say to us. The Bible is an integral part of our spiritual life in this world.

The Bible is actually God's perspective on our world. This is the way he sees things. You have to give him credit for knowing what he's talking about! He created the world, so certainly he knows how it works and where its shortcomings are. He also knows how far off it is

---

[1] The number of references to this idea in the Bible are too numerous to list here; my personal favorite is Paul's statement to the Thessalonians – "And we also thank God continually because, when you received the ***Word of God***, which you heard from us, you accepted it not as the word of men, but as it actually is, the ***Word of God***, which is at work in you who believe." (1 Thessalonians 2:13) He is commending them for believing that the Bible really is the Word of God and not falling prey to the doubts that many have about it.

from the original pattern. He can see clearly how broken it is, how we've twisted it into our own playground of lust, power and greed.

God also founded the physical world on spiritual realities – which we would never know about unless he told us. The Bible shows us these realities. We can't escape justice, or Judgment Day, or the spiritual cause-and-effect that he built into the world. "The soul that sins shall die." "The wages of sin is death." These spiritual realities are more real than the sun coming up.

In the Bible, God also reveals his agenda for this world and his new Kingdom that he is building. We know from what we read that he is "raising up nations and tearing down nations." He is going to "shake the created world" and get rid of everything that doesn't directly support his new spiritual Kingdom. We read of the rules of the coming Kingdom, and the qualities that are necessary if one wants to be a citizen there. Though we don't see these things in the world around us, the Bible shines a light on God's special works and tells us plainly what is coming. Nobody will be without excuse when the end comes.

Our culture tells us none of these things. People are living in total darkness, as if none of this is real. So in our day it has become a battle of authorities: unbelievers don't believe that anything that the Bible says is true, and Christians can see clearly through their faith that it is true. Only time will prove it.

The Bible is such a vital resource for your spiritual survival, that the enemies of God have mounted overwhelming attacks against it in our modern times. The argument is that the Bible is an old-fashioned, out-of-date document that is unreliable at best. Unfortunately most churches, and almost all colleges, universities and seminaries, teach their students that the Bible isn't reliable. They are preparing these people for failure. But having been through three seminaries and hundreds of books on the subject, I can assure you that these criticisms are empty and without foundation. The only reason these critics don't believe the Bible is because they *don't want* to believe it. There's absolutely no basis in the Bible for their criticisms. The Bible is, as Jesus, the Apostles and the Prophets claimed of it, the Word of God to man's heart and mind – just as it stands.

Keep in mind that we are at war. The enemy will use anything to turn us away from God and truth – even the very institutions that claim to serve God!

Trusting God's Word is going to be an important survival skill for God's people. What we need is faith and the right attitude.

- **Faith** – because we have to *see* that this is truly God's Word, the only truth that enlightens us, the foundation of our lives, the only description of the road to Heaven.

- **The right attitude** – because we must submit to God's Word, never doubt it, and trust it implicitly like a child.

There are going to be many times in life when the Bible will be the *only* thing we have to go on. We would really love to have a sign drop down out of Heaven, or a miracle pop out of the ground, but nothing like that happens. The only foundation that we have to stand on is what the Bible says to us. This is living by faith alone – trusting and believing in what God says in his Word, in spite of appearances. It's that quiet confidence that the truth of God is more true than what we see in this world. Persevere in *that*, and he will reward you. It's easy to live on miracles, but it's not easy at all to live by faith in the Word.

> Because you have seen me, you have believed; blessed are those who have not seen and yet have believed. (John 20:29)

Students learn their lessons in a classroom, where everything is peaceful, quiet and abstract. They almost never think ahead to the times when they will use this knowledge they are getting. It looks so simple on the blackboard! When they get out on the job, however, in a real-life situation, it doesn't always hit them that they are looking at that formula or principle that they learned back in school.

Surrounded by trials, our friends leaving us, family proving treacherous, loss of security, health and goods, indoctrinated by an unbelieving world, tempted to turn aside from our path and take an easier road, no hope and no light to give us encouragement – only the person well-trained in spiritual survival will know the principles from the Bible that apply to this situation. We have to be able to transfer abstract truth to a real-world problem. Not everyone can do this; it takes a lot of training and thought.

What makes the situation worse is that we tend to seize up and panic when things fall apart. Our emotions tend to get in the way – fear, for one – and we weaken in our determination to follow God in his difficult ways. We forget our lessons; we don't realize that we learned what to do in this situation in the comfort of the Sunday School class or Bible study. The survivor will go to the Word, and stick to the Word *no matter what happens,* and persevere in its plain and simple truth, no matter how confusing or distressing the situation. Even if the Bible contradicts everything and everyone around us. Of course we all know that we have to do this to survive, but it's a difficult thing to carry out in the middle of the battle.

> If your Law had not been my delight, I would have
> perished in my affliction. I will never forget your precepts,
> for by them you have preserved my life. (Psalm 119:92-93)

So, a spiritual survivor makes understanding the Bible his primary objective. He works on it *before* hard times come, when he has the time, energy, and a clear mind for it. He will carry it with him, like notes from the classroom, through the confusion of battle and follow it with complete trust. The Bible shows him the resources to ask for, and the procedures to follow, in times of need. It is God's instructions for leading the child of God through this world and to himself.

Led by the Spirit

Besides the Word, one of the most precious resources that the Christian has is the Spirit of Christ.

> But the Counselor, the Holy Spirit, whom the Father
> will send in my name, will teach you all things and will
> remind you of everything I have said to you. (John 14:26)

Though we may understand what the Bible says about spiritual realities, living as though they are real will require the work of the

Spirit on our minds and hearts. Since God *wants* us to know him, he's not going to let us flounder around helplessly, wondering how we're going to do it. As soon as we become believers, he gives us his Spirit.

> I keep asking that the God of our Lord Jesus Christ, the glorious Father, may give you the Spirit of wisdom and revelation, so that you may know him better. (Ephesians 1:17)

We are about to walk into a strange world, a world that our physical senses won't be able to pick up on. The Spirit will do two things for us so that we can see God's world.

First, the Spirit *reveals* the world of God to us.

> "No eye has seen, no ear has heard, no mind has conceived what God has prepared for those who love him" – but God has revealed it to us by his Spirit … We have not received the spirit of the world but the Spirit who is from God, that we may understand what God has freely given us. (1 Corinthians 2:9-10, 12)

All the saints of the Old Testament who had faith could see God's spiritual world by means of the physical lessons that God gave them. They were lifted up, by the Spirit, out of this world, beyond the physical, into spiritual realities. What they saw there were the eternal treasures in Christ, just as clearly as we see them today. In fact, they witnessed firsthand the realities that we Christians usually only read about in our Bibles. Hebrews assures us of this.

> All these people were still living by faith when they died. They did not receive the things promised; they only saw them and welcomed them from a distance. And they admitted that they were aliens and strangers on earth. People who say such things show that they are looking for a country of their own. If they had been thinking of the country they had left, they would have had opportunity to return. Instead, they were longing for a better country – a Heavenly one. Therefore God is not ashamed to be called

their God, for he has prepared a city for them. (Hebrews 11:13-16)

By faith he left Egypt, not fearing the king's anger; he persevered because he saw him who is invisible. (Hebrews 11:27)

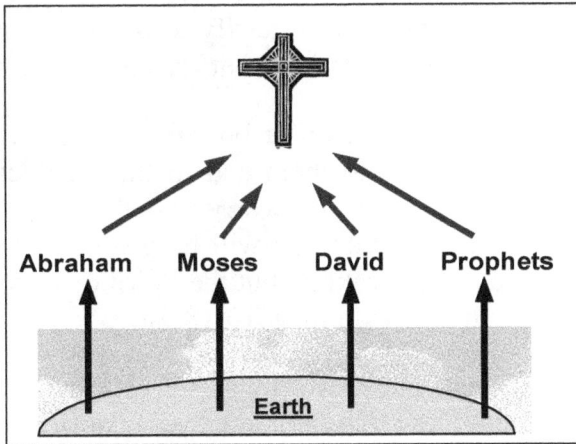

Faith sees the eternal Christ

Remember that Jesus told us that the Spirit always works hand in hand with the Word. He takes what we read there and ushers us into its reality. He never reveals anything to us that isn't in the Word of God – Old *and* New Testaments. The Word reveals God; the Spirit brings us into his presence.

Second, the Spirit *empowers* us to use the things of God's world. The Spirit gives us a new power that helps us do the impossible.

> But you will receive power when the Holy Spirit comes on you; and you will be my witnesses in Jerusalem, and in all Judea and Samaria, and to the ends of the earth. (Acts 1:8)

By the Spirit we are enabled to "take hold of the promises," to "lay up treasures in Heaven," to boldly enter the Temple in Heaven with confidence to lay our requests before the Father.

Let us draw near to God with a sincere heart in full assurance of faith, having our hearts sprinkled to cleanse us from a guilty conscience and having our bodies washed with pure water. (Hebrews 10:22)

We not only find ourselves able to enjoy the good things of God, but we are also filled with power from God to go back to our lives enabled to walk with Christ, and to testify to others by our words and actions about the spiritual foundations that are now under our feet.

On my account you will be brought before governors and kings as witnesses to them and to the Gentiles. But when they arrest you, do not worry about what to say or how to say it. At that time you will be given what to say, for it will not be you speaking, but the Spirit of your Father speaking through you. (Matthew 10:18-20)

When the Spirit does these two things for us, God becomes real in our lives. Our religion isn't a dry, intellectual, historical pastime, but a life with God. We will experience what Enoch of old experienced.

Enoch walked with God. (Genesis 5:24)

The Spirit, then, is leading us back to God, to make us God-centered.

When you follow the leading of the Spirit, you will find the reality of God's life filling you from the inside, as Jesus predicted.

Whoever drinks the water I give him will never thirst. Indeed, the water I give him will become in him a spring of water welling up to eternal life. (John 4:14)

The new nature of Christ, the New Man, will begin taking you over. Little do you realize at this point how life-saving that change will be! God's wrath will be poured out on the wicked; if he sees the nature of Christ in you, however, he will "pass over" you in his wrath. What he sees in you is the fruit of holiness that so pleases him.

But the fruit of the Spirit is love, joy, peace, patience, kindness, goodness, faithfulness, gentleness and self-control. Against such things there is no law. Those who belong to Christ Jesus have crucified the sinful nature with its passions and desires. Since we live by the Spirit, let us keep in step with the Spirit. (Galatians 5:22-25)

So, the Spirit enables us to live and survive *spiritually*, in *God's* world – where survival really counts. He's going to crucify our flesh, and lead us away from this world, because survival in this world isn't nearly as important on God's agenda. Losing our lives here isn't the terror for Christians that it is for unbelievers; it's actually the open door to Heaven.

If anyone would come after me, he must deny himself and take up his cross and follow me. For whoever wants to save his life will lose it, but whoever loses his life for me will find it. (Matthew 16:24-25)

The person who can successfully follow the Spirit will find life, not death, in the strange and difficult paths that he uses to lead us to God.

Mastering the Bible

To know God is life. (John 17:3) And God gave the Bible to his people so that they could know him. Therefore, to read, study, and meditate on the Bible is the same thing as breathing, spiritually speaking. We can't live without the Bible.

It's unfortunate that so many people, even in the church, pretty much ignore the Bible. I know that they read a few verses here and there (mainly their favorite promises), and a little bit of the Bible gets pumped into their heads during worship services. But that's not the same thing as studying it on their own. It's as if their only exposure to the Bible are the times when it's done to them, like artificial respiration. They're not breathing on their own.

Crucial for life

The world is made up of two realities: the physical and the spiritual. God wisely set the physical world in a spiritual framework, so that our actions in this world will be guided by spiritual principles.

But it takes faith to see this spiritual framework. Not only must God open our eyes so that we can see (by means of the work of the

Spirit), but he must then reveal that world to us. That revelation is the Bible. Here we have open windows into God's house, and we can see the spiritual realities that hold our physical world together. Now we can know that there's a reason for God's laws over us. Now we know why it's important to follow his rules; they are guidelines that help us navigate through an otherwise dark, bewildering world.

This information is all laid out for us in the Bible, because there is no other place we can get it. *This is the sole source of information about God.*

Like students at school, then, we have to learn the lessons from the Bible well enough that, when we need it later in life, we can bring those lessons back to mind and use what we know. This is why the Bible tells us to store up this information in our minds.

> I have hidden your Word in my heart that I might not sin against you. (Psalm 119:11)

> Wise men store up knowledge, but the mouth of a fool invites ruin. (Proverbs 10:14)

> The heart of the discerning acquires knowledge; the ears of the wise seek it out. (Proverbs 18:15)

In fact, though at first we may not appreciate the treasure we have in the Bible, the value of it grows on us over time and with use. We start seeing how vital it is to see this spiritual world – it explains so much about why things work the way they do. It helps us avoid pitfalls that others fall into blindly. The Word leads us to God, to peace and joy, when everything else around us is so confusing. God's truth *works*. And as we begin to rely on it more and more, we begin to ask God for more light, more truth, more knowledge and wisdom; the picture gets clearer and clearer.

> Your Word is a lamp to my feet and a light for my path. (Psalm 119:105)

> Do good to your servant according to your Word, O LORD. (Psalm 119:65)

But his delight is in the Law of the LORD, and on his Law he meditates day and night. He is like a tree planted by streams of water, which yields its fruit in season and whose leaf does not wither. Whatever he does prospers. (Psalm 1:2-3)

All of the Bible is a clear path to God. Jesus, for example, told the story about Lazarus ending up in Heaven with Abraham, and the rich man ended up in Hell. When the rich man wanted to send a messenger to his family to warn them about the reality of Hell, Abraham answered him like this:

They have Moses and the Prophets; let them listen to them. (Luke 16:29)

I hope you realize what Jesus is saying here. The very part of the Bible that people most often ignore – the Old Testament – is the key to salvation. The *whole Bible* is the doorway to life.

You may or may not have someone to help you with this. In many churches, people are content to let the preacher do the eating for them; all they want to taste is a little bit of what the preacher has chewed up for them (like a baby bird in the nest!). There are many preachers who are all too willing to do this for people, since it feeds their sense of power and control over a group of people.

You're not going to get to Heaven that way; neither will you be able to survive in times of disaster and trouble. If that is your church situation, you're going to have to strike out on your own and do your own work. Your soul is at stake here. *You* must get into the Bible, learn it, master it, and live by it. Nobody can do this for you. Only in times of trouble will most people finally find out whether they are able to lean directly on God, or whether they are followers of men.

The Revelation of God

When you study the Bible, the most important point to keep in mind is that *it is the revelation of God*. The Bible has all sorts of information in it, but you will always miss its meaning if you keep chasing down rabbit trails and side issues. Look for God in this book!

Scientists and scholars do a wonderful job of describing our physical world to us; they use windows, like telescopes and microscopes, to peer into that world. But they can't show us God and his spiritual world; that's where the Bible comes in. This is the *only* window to God and his world that we have. Here God reveals what we could never have found out on our own.

The word "revelation" means to uncover something so that we can see it. It's an act of God; it's not something that man can do. When God reveals himself, we discover that he's not at all like other "gods" that we imagined. This God is unique; this God is real.

So when we read the Bible, it requires a certain attitude. We come to *learn*. This is no time for pride or arrogance. We have no knowledge about God before he teaches us; we are all like little children when we come to the Bible.

> Guard your steps when you go to the house of God. Go
> near to listen rather than to offer the sacrifice of fools, who
> do not know that they do wrong. (Ecclesiastes 5:1)

At every step, we are going to learn the truth about God that we need to know to survive in this world. He's going to show us a great deal about ourselves, too, that we didn't know – which will be humbling. He isn't going to teach us what we *want* to know, but what we *need* to know. For example, when Isaiah saw God in his Temple, the thing that struck him was the utter holiness of God and how unrighteous we all are compared to him.

> In the year that King Uzziah died, I saw the Lord seated
> on a throne, high and exalted, and the train of his robe
> filled the temple. Above him were seraphs, each with six
> wings: With two wings they covered their faces, with two
> they covered their feet, and with two they were flying. And
> they were calling to one another: "Holy, holy, holy is the
> LORD Almighty; the whole earth is full of his glory." At
> the sound of their voices the doorposts and thresholds

shook and the temple was filled with smoke. "Woe to me!" I cried. "I am ruined! For I am a man of unclean lips, and I live among a people of unclean lips, and my eyes have seen the King, the LORD Almighty." (Isaiah 6:1-5)

You know that you're learning something vital about God when you read a passage in the Bible and it shakes you. You didn't know that God was like this. You didn't know that God sees you as unrighteous compared to himself. You didn't know that God's commands are designed to lead you out of your sin and into righteousness. The Bible enlightens you, teaches you, and opens the door into the spiritual world that makes the picture much clearer to see. That's why we need it so much.

The Bible shows us God in his true light. We learn what God is really like as –

- *The Judge* – He sees our hearts to their depths; he doesn't need to hear our pitiful excuses for our behavior. He measures our actions, our very thoughts and feelings, by setting his Law against us like a yardstick – and finds that we fall short of his eternal standards. When you stand before this Judge, you realize what a terrible position that your sin has put you in. The fear of God suddenly becomes real to you; it's no longer an academic idea. Read the Prophets sometime and you will begin to experience what it's like to stand before the Judge. There isn't anything about you that he doesn't know.

- *The Creator* – He made the entire universe through his Word and by miracle. He made it with infinite wisdom; everything fits together perfectly and is under his direct, unerring control. He cares for it daily; he makes sure his creatures have food to eat and air to breathe. There isn't anything that this God can't do. When we study the works of this God as he controls his world and directs its course, it becomes obvious to us that this is a God we can trust completely with our lives. Surely he knows what we are made of! He knows what we need, and when we need it. We can let him take care of the details of our needs.

- ***The Father*** – He opened up his heart to us in his Son Jesus Christ. Now we know what God will do for his children. He opens the door to his house and invites us all the way in to his throne. He opens up the storehouses of his treasures in Heaven and invites us to take whatever we need. He draws us close, in Jesus, and reveals a love that forgives us of our sins and accepts us into his family. He blesses his children with joy unspeakable – his unmeasured goodness. We will grow to love this God who so loves us.

If this is the way you use the Bible – to find God – then God will begin to show himself to you.

> And you, my son Solomon, acknowledge the God of your father, and serve him with wholehearted devotion and with a willing mind, for the LORD searches every heart and understands every motive behind the thoughts. If you seek him, he will be found by you; but if you forsake him, he will reject you forever. (1 Chronicles 28:9)

Overview of the Bible

In order to appreciate the Bible and get the most out of it, you have to approach it methodically. The Bible is so big, and it's made up of thousands of stories and characters. You can easily get lost in the forest if you don't do some preliminary work. First you have to get the "big picture" if you want to start putting together its pieces.

The Bible has *one* message: God created mankind upright, or righteous, and gave him the job of ruling over his creation according to his Law. But man rebelled against God's rule over him; he now lives apart from God. The result has been death and destruction, ruin and misery. For most of mankind, the future is dark: God plans to destroy the wicked in eternal punishment. But for a chosen few, God has plans to bring them back to life – spiritual life (which is knowing God) – and lift them up even higher than man's original calling. He plans to make man one with his own Son, Jesus Christ, and seat man beside him by his throne in Heaven. In other words, God is going to save these people of his from their sin and death and give them eternal life.

The entire Bible deals with this plan of salvation. Both the Old and New Testaments lay out the plan in detail.

When you boil down the Bible to its simplest level, it actually covers three things: the **Problem**, which describes why we have such a terrible relationship with the God who made us; the **Solution Described**, which shows how God intends to solve our problem for his glory and our eternal benefit; and the **Solution Applied**, in which God takes the finished plan and starts saving people from their problem.

The Problem   **The Solution Described**   **The Solution Applied**

The Problem: Genesis 1-11

The Bible starts out by describing the fundamental problem of humanity. But in order to do this, it first starts with the Creation of the world. Here we learn *who* made the world, *how* he made it, and *why* he made it.

God made the world, we are told in Genesis, and we learn right away that he is holy and righteous. So he designed the entire world to show off his holiness; all his creatures are designed and expected to glorify him. He is also the King, ruling the universe from his throne in Heaven. This means that all creatures were made to serve him, according to his specific rules. His rules are what we call righteousness, or the Law.

There are more things about God that we can learn from Genesis, but just these two points are enough to set the background for the problem to come. In Genesis 3 we find out that Adam and Eve rebelled against the King and turned their back on his holiness. In that act of rebellion, they brought down the entire human race into disaster. Now all of their children would inherit their sin nature. God responded with a sentence of death as a just punishment against Adam and his race. Now instead of a happy communion between God and man, there is war. And there doesn't appear to be any chance of a reconciliation, since God closed the doors to Heaven and eternal life.

The problem gets worse – or perhaps we should say that we can see the true extent and seriousness of the problem as the story unfolds. The first murder occurs in Genesis 4, teaching us what man is capable of doing to his fellow man out of selfishness and jealousy. In Genesis 6-9 we are told that all of humanity is wallowing in sin; the situation was so bad that God decided to sweep the planet clean and start over with Noah (at least one person had true faith!) and his immediate family. Then in Genesis 11 we see the entire world back in sin, challenging God's authority over them, and building the Tower of Babel as a symbol of rebellion and independence. God scattered them over the whole earth and took away their ability to work together against him.

So the situation, described in the first 11 chapters of the Bible, is this: Heaven and earth are at war with each other, and there doesn't appear to be any hope that we're going to survive this war. Mankind is determined to rebel against God and have its own way; God is just as determined to stop man, wiping him out entirely if necessary, to stay in control of the situation. We are faced with an impasse. If something isn't done, we're all doomed. The only one who can make a move to break the impasse at this point is God.

We need Genesis 1-11 to show us the nature of the problem (treason against God), the extent of the problem (in every human being world-wide), and how seriously God takes it (death is the punishment). At least we all know now where we stand with our Maker. And we know now that there's nothing *we* can do to fix the problem.

The Solution Described: Genesis 12 – John

There *is* a second solution to mankind's problem – besides wholesale destruction.   Without relaxing his standards, God introduced a way of forgiving our sin against him and delivering us from any further sin. He's going to re-open the way to the Tree of Life, but on his terms.

This solution is staggering, to say the least. God is going to do things that people would never have imagined. Even the angels, who are God's messengers and closest to the Throne of Heaven, would be kept in the dark until the whole solution unfolds. The job at hand is to completely free the sinner from condemnation, yet satisfy the righteous requirements of the Law, and make sure that sin would never happen again – the whole time changing man's heart so that he *wants* to cooperate with God in this venture. So the answer that God provides is going to be astonishing and complex; it's going to require thousands of years to complete.

The Lord described and worked out the solution in stages. First came the Promise, the Covenant, with Abraham and his descendants, starting with Genesis 12. Throughout the entire history of the Jews (as described in the Old Testament), God worked out the Solution. Keep in mind that he worked on parts of the solution at different periods of Israel's history, but the entire pattern was already complete in Heaven. There was never any doubt about where he was going. He knew from the beginning where he wanted to end up. We are shown no more than a glimpse of the solution in any particular story, but each bit is a precious and vital step in our salvation. To the perceptive Jew, the parts added up to a whole picture of God's salvation of mankind.

Another method that God used was the idea of "shadows." Instead of directly revealing the Kingdom of Heaven that will be our eternal home, he cast shadows of that spiritual world on the earth. The Jews had to work with those shadows, not the real thing. They were told about this, and they were expected to know that true faith would trust in the real spiritual world behind the physical land, the Temple, and the animal sacrifices. But the shadows played their role in the process of salvation, because we can more easily learn from what we see and feel than from invisible concepts.

What this means is that each thing that happened in the Old Testament wasn't an imperfect picture, but rather a small piece of the picture. We need to put all the pieces together to see the whole picture. The New Testament isn't the mature statement over against the "childish" or immature religion of the Jews (as some critics claim). The New Testament simply goes back to the Old Testament, collects all the pieces, and lifts it up into God's spiritual world – a resurrection of sorts. The physical body becomes a spiritual body in the New Testament. And the Old Testament pattern, filled with the light of Christ, finally makes sense.

To truly understand the story of Jesus, we first need to do our homework in the history of the Israelites. Jesus was symbolized in many forms, each of which teaches us a different facet of the Son of God. For example, he is portrayed in the Passover meal in Exodus as the spotless Lamb offered for our sake so that we might not be destroyed. Revelation 5 confirms him as a Lamb on the throne. Everyone knows that Jesus isn't a literal (animal) lamb; what we need to learn is *why* he is shown as a Lamb – the answer is in the Old Testament.

Even when Jesus appeared in the Gospels, God was still working out the finishing touches of the system. People were supposed to watch and learn, but the time had not yet come when they would experience the full weight of the power of

God's salvation in their hearts. They could only wait for that reality.

The Solution Applied: Acts – Revelation

When Jesus said from the cross, "It is finished," he was speaking of the great system that God had been putting together in the Bible until that moment. Now the time had come to start applying the salvation that the Old Testament describes in the hearts of individuals.

We find out right away that God meant it to be a spiritual solution. He did away with the physical that he used to teach the Israelites; they must now grow up and start thinking in spiritual terms. The blood of bulls and goats, we are told, never was enough to cleanse our hearts of sin. It was only meant to teach us the utter seriousness of sin (death is the penalty), and God's mercy in providing an alternate victim for our sin. So God destroyed the Temple, the sacrificial system, and everything else that the Jews were relying on for their salvation.

Also we learn the method that God is going to use to accomplish what couldn't be done even in the Old Testament days. Though the Israelites had learned the truth of God's plan of salvation, they still lacked the motive power – they remained sinners after all their prayers and sacrifices. But now Jesus will send his Holy Spirit to live inside us. That power will bring about the heart-change that God requires of his people. God's people have longed for this step, even from the Old Testament days.

There are many things that the Holy Spirit will enable us to do. All these things were first described in the Old Testament, of course. The Spirit will enable us to ascend to the Throne of God in Heaven, enter his Temple, and personally present our prayers and requests to him. The Spirit will break our hearts of stone and move us to follow his decrees and laws. The Spirit will defend us from our enemies. The Spirit will bring us to a land of peace, fill our lives with "milk and honey," and make us a testimony to the nations surrounding us. What the Jews wished they could do but couldn't, Christians now are able to do.

The end result is astonishing. In Christ, who has gone before us (he makes every single step in this process work for us), we will ascend to the throne of God himself as priests and sit at his right hand as his children. There we will rule over his new Heavens and earth *as we were designed to do at the beginning*. But there won't be any second fall into sin and death. Being one with the Son of God, we will be pure and holy forever. And we will actually *like* it that way!

By looking at the Bible in this way – **Problem**, **Solution Described**, and **Solution Applied** – we get a feel for God's great work of salvation throughout history. It's one project, one plan, bringing all of God's people into his eternal Kingdom. Paul describes it like this:

There is one body and one Spirit – just as you were called to one hope when you were called – one Lord, one faith, one baptism; one God and Father of all, who is over all and through all and in all. (Ephesians 4:4-6)

We know of course that history consists of much more than the Bible's narrow focus. After reading Greek and Roman history, and the full history of the Egyptians, and the history of Medieval Europe, and all of modern history, we realize that the little bit of history that the Bible talks about is actually a miniscule part of all human endeavor. Most of humanity, unfortunately, will never know the blessings that are described in the Bible's story of salvation. The Bible is not their story. God has another plan for those who take the "wide road" of sin – the terrible day of Judgment and the Lake of Fire.

But for a few, the Bible describes their future: it's about God providing a way of escape from the day of wrath. While the rest of the world concerns itself with *this* world which eventually will be destroyed, the children of God are following a different track. They are being prepared for life in the *new* world in Heaven that the Bible describes.

Once you see this message across the entire Bible, you can start fitting the details of the Bible into that message. Things will make sense to you as you see them in light of God's plan of salvation.

Another way we can show this is by the following chart:

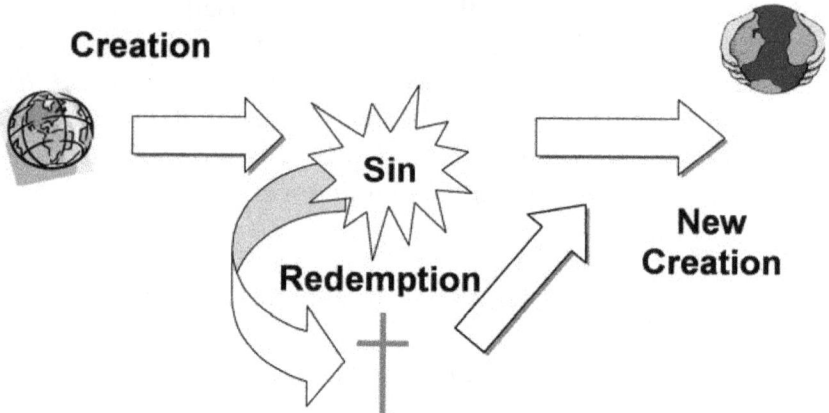

In the beginning, God created a perfect world and had every intention of blessing man and enabling him to rule over his earth in his Name. Sin, however, blew apart that arrangement. God refused to go on in such circumstances. But rather than simply do away with the whole thing and call it quits, he took an alternate route – one in which he would personally suffer on our account, so that a few of us would be saved from the disaster that mankind brought upon itself. Once Jesus bought reconciliation with God through his death, and opened the way to eternal life through his resurrection, man was brought back to his Maker (and his Redeemer!) and set back on the path to eternal life. When everyone that God saves is brought back to him, he will put them in a new Heaven and earth where they will live with God forever, as originally planned. Only now there won't be any chance of going back to sin and death, because God will have his hands on us – we will be safe in Christ – forever.

Once you have this "big picture" view of the Bible, you know what the real issues of life are: God's glory, our sin and death, the way back to God in Christ. You will know exactly why God gave you his Book and what he expects you to do with it. This keeps you from wasting your time following "rabbit trails" and spending so much time on matters that are secondary. Work on the "one thing needful" – the great Mission of getting you ready to live with God.

The Old and New Testaments

For a little while we had to set aside the distinction between "Old" and "New" Testaments, so that we could get the full picture of the Bible. It's really one story, not two. Now we want to draw the line between them again, but this time we're not going to set one against another but see how one complements the other. They are like two sides of the same coin.

So let's gather a few key Scriptures together and find the fundamental lesson of the Old Testament. First, we discover that the Old Testament was veiled to the average person:

> We are not like Moses, who would put a veil over his face to keep the Israelites from gazing at it while the radiance was fading away. But their minds were made dull, for to this day the same veil remains when the old covenant is read. It has not been removed, because only in Christ is it taken away. Even to this day when Moses is read, a veil covers their hearts. But whenever anyone turns to the Lord, the veil is taken away. (2 Corinthians 3:13-16)

The Old Testament contained a mystery. It was the eternal message of God to man, but it was temporarily shrouded in physical dress. The Jews were selected out of all the nations on earth to learn the truth about the only God. However, they had a severe problem on their hands: whereas the "gods" of other nations were easy to see (since they were idols of wood and stone and metal), the Jewish God was invisible. In fact, they were not allowed to represent him in any way with the things of earth! (See Exodus 20:4-5 for this command.) So how does one find out what an invisible God is like? The way that God chose is typical of a good educator: he used pictures to teach them.

> In the past God spoke to our forefathers through the prophets at many times and in various ways. (Hebrews 1:1)

Through the events of history, and the great personalities of Israel, God taught them how to be saved from sin and death. This is, after all, the great need of mankind; the Old Testament teaches us this fundamental lesson in "story book" fashion. The fascinating thing about this is that we Christians can now look back through the Old Testament and recognize our New Testament doctrines all through its stories! Obviously God had the big picture of salvation in view when he laid out the events of Israel's history in his plans. In other words, he gave the Jews the first version of the story of Christ.

That means that the two books – the Old and the New Testaments – tell the *same story*. The first version was told to a people living in the middle of a wicked, ignorant world; the Israelites needed help to understand a God they couldn't see. After the story was told completely over their 2000-year history, it went into its second version in the New Testament. Now that we have learned the plot of the story, God is going to lift us Christians up to the spiritual reality that the first version of the story pointed to.

I hope you can see by now that God knew that, without the first physical version of the story, we would never understand the second spiritual version. It's like reading a map. If we first study the map before we go somewhere, we will recognize the real roads and terrain when we get there. The Old Testament was the map for our New Testament real-life experiences in Christ.

God didn't always tell the Israelites where they were headed with all this. He deliberately kept it a secret, a "mystery," to be revealed at a later date. The way that *we* know what he was doing back then are the plain statements about it in the New Testament. Still, there was something about the Old Testament system that left (or *should* have left!) the Jews wondering – this seemed to be pointing to something important! For instance, when God told them to build a tabernacle in which to worship him, he said this:

Then have them make a sanctuary for me, and I will dwell among them. Make this tabernacle and all its furnishings exactly like the pattern I will show you. (Exodus 25:8-9)

But Solomon, after he had built the permanent Temple in Jerusalem, knew that an earthly structure (no matter how glorious) couldn't hold the eternal God:

But will God really dwell on earth with men? The heavens, even the highest heavens, cannot contain you. How much less this temple I have built! (2 Chronicles 6:18)

Some of them had faith – they could see the spiritual Temple in Heaven. They knew that the physical Temple was actually an earthly copy to introduce the Israelites to the worship of God the easy way.

They serve at a sanctuary that is a copy and shadow of what is in Heaven. This is why Moses was warned when he was about to build the tabernacle: "See to it that you make everything according to the pattern shown you on the mountain." (Hebrews 8:5)

We Christians know, from the extensive descriptions found particularly in Paul's letters and Hebrews, that the Temple and its sacrificial system are great descriptions of Christ and his sacrifice. Do you see where we are going with this? Without saying as much, the Old Testament story describes Christ and his work in great detail. The Jews had inside information about Jesus long before the rest of the world did. The name "Jesus" was never written in any of the stories, and only once in a while was there a clue that all of this referred to the Messiah to come. Basically God kept telling his people, "Trust me – you'll see all of this later, and it will make perfect sense then."

In fact, every story of the Old Testament has this great aim in view: *to describe Jesus Christ, and our relationship to God the Father through him.* Christians have always known that there is a lot of prophetic material about Christ in the Old Testament, and a few symbols and types here and there. But let's back up another step. The very history of the book, the lives and characters portrayed there, the forces and dynamic flow of the principles involved, all help to complete a grand unified (and very detailed) picture of Jesus and his work. By the time we get to the New Testament, we should already know all about him. The only thing left to be done is to lift our eyes to the spiritual level that the physical pointed to.

> The Law is only a shadow of the good things that are coming – not the realities themselves. (Hebrews 10:1)

In fact, the writers of the New Testament purposely refrain from going over the same material that was in the Old Testament. They figured that you have already done your homework and are ready for the next level.

> We have much to say about this, but it is hard to explain because you are slow to learn. In fact, though by this time you ought to be teachers, you need someone to teach you the elementary truths of God's word all over again. You need milk, not solid food! (Hebrews 5:11-12)

Following this complaint, the writer of Hebrews lists a number of doctrines that we should already be familiar with, truths first learned in the Old Testament. This is also why Paul was so certain that we can learn all we need to know about salvation through Christ by studying the *Old* Testament.

> ... and how from infancy you have known the holy Scriptures [*the **Old** Testament!*], which are able to make you wise for salvation through faith in Christ Jesus. (2 Timothy 3:15)

The New Testament is a highly condensed, complex description of Christ. Now that we're on a spiritual level, there is much more to learn about him and incorporate into our lives if we're to be ready for Heaven. But *are* we ready? To fully appreciate these higher spiritual truths, we have to be well-grounded in the fundamental truths about Christ. Jesus is the foundation of the entire Church, Old and New Testament. He has thousands of functions in God's Kingdom, and scores of names that describe his personality and works. Many things about him are best described by looking at real-life experiences in people's lives. In light of all this, it's no wonder that God chose to fully tell the story about him over a period of 2000 years, through the lives of millions of people, across a book that makes up fully three-fourths of our current Bible! It couldn't be done in a shorter span.

It can't be sidestepped without doing great harm to one's understanding of who Christ is. Christians who don't know anything about the Old Testament are crippled in their understanding of Christ. It's true that they may have the germ of salvation in their minds (and hopefully their hearts), but that's because God is merciful and works with us according to our circumstances (which in these lean spiritual times will mean ill-equipped Christians). The problem is that we are Gentiles who have been brought into a new world, a world that only the Jews have had any formal training in. God made us alive in Christ, it's true; but with *only* that feather in our cap we can hardly claim to be experts on God and his Word! Now is the time for training and teaching, so that "we all reach unity in the faith and in the knowledge of the Son of God and become mature, attaining to the whole measure of the *fullness* of Christ." (Ephesians 4:13)

So our goal here is to ask the question: What does the Old Testament teach me about Jesus Christ? If we keep that question before us as we read it, we will be looking for the right lesson in its pages, the one thing it was designed to teach us. We will be turning our ears and hearts to God, who wants to tell us this very thing. Aiming at any other goal while studying the Old Testament is missing its point.

There are actually only two *new* concepts that the New Testament deals with, things that the Old Testament saints had never dreamed of. In fact these two things caught the Jews completely off guard; they stumbled over these two points. In themselves they are staggering concepts, so it's no wonder that the entire New Testament is devoted to them. They are the finishing touch to God's system of salvation that was so laboriously developed in the Old Testament. The Apostles (by means of the Spirit of God) grasped the importance of these two points and how necessary they are to finish and even make possible the solution to sin and death. Without them the great Jewish system would have ground to a halt; with them, it becomes Christianity.

The point of the New Testament can be put like this:

The New Testament reveals the New Man, and how we become one with him.

God's sole aim throughout history was the restoration of man. What he wants is for us to be perfect again, as he originally designed us. In the Old Testament he worked out a plan that will erase our past, purify our hearts, and make us fit to live with him forever. What was lacking, however, was the motive power that would make it work. The Jews, even knowing all the details about salvation, never succeeded in following all the necessary steps. Everyone failed God somewhere along the line, in some way.

So God did it himself. The *first new concept* that the New Testament has for us is that God became a man. The incarnation of Christ was something that the Old Testament never described in doctrinal form as it does the rest of our faith. That's why the Jews reacted so violently against Jesus' statements about having come from his Father in Heaven. But it was a vital step in the plan, because without it we could never be saved from sin and death. We knew that God planned to solve our problem by himself from several key Old Testament passages (for example, see Isaiah 63:6), but becoming a man was a surprise.

This is in fact a testing point – a Shibboleth, if you will – of our faith. The true Christian says the right things about Jesus.

> This is how you can recognize the Spirit of God: *Every spirit that acknowledges that Jesus Christ has come in the flesh is from God,* but every spirit that does not acknowledge Jesus is not from God. This is the spirit of the antichrist, which you have heard is coming and even now is already in the world. (1 John 4:2-3)

This New Man enters the Bible in the Gospels full of the power of the Spirit, which was the motive force that was necessary to make the Old Testament system work. Jesus obeyed the Law to the letter, to its very depths; this is something that God has wanted to see a man do since the beginning of time. Jesus loved his Father and lived solely to do his will. He loved men and worked day and night for their physical and spiritual benefit. He hated sin. He fought the enemy with the power of the Spirit and won all confrontations. He was filled with wisdom and insight. His entire life was holy – that is, set apart for God's use alone.

Nobody else could have done this as the Son of God did. For thousands of years the Jews tried and failed to please God living under the Law. But Jesus was different. In a single lifetime he achieved what generations of Israelites couldn't do before him. "This is my Son, whom I love; with him I am well pleased." (Matthew 3:17)

Now that a perfect life had been lived according to the high standards of God's Law, Jesus could pay the price for our sins. His death, the death of a righteous man, was the sacrifice that finally appeased the wrath of God against sinners. A substitute (which the Law allows, because of the mercy of God) took our punishment upon himself so that we might be set free from condemnation. Again, this is not a concept that could be developed in the Old Testament. No man's life was precious enough to God to substitute for ours; only the life of the Son of God would move God's heart and cleanse ours.

To finish the job, God raised Jesus from the dead into eternal life, and lifted him high above all things in the universe to his own right hand, sitting on the throne of Heaven. Now a *man* sits as co-regent with God! The resurrection of Christ wasn't just for his own sake, but was a key step in *our* salvation. It's not as if Jesus wanted to do any of this for his own benefit; he already had a perfect life with the Father before the world was made. He became a man so that *we* might become one with God. He did this so that we might be saved.

That's the **second concept that is new** in the New Testament. The Old Testament continually preached the need for us to be holy, righteous, and to live for the will of God – but it never even hinted that God would do something staggering to make it possible for us to go to Heaven to be his children. To make sure we become holy and stay that way forever, God's solution is to make us *one with Christ* the Holy One, his Son. We have become part of his very body, his life. Now we can't fail! Now wherever Jesus goes, we go with him; whatever he does, we do with him. He became heir of God's Kingdom, and so do we who are united with him. He became the second Adam, the firstborn of a new race destined for the Throne of Heaven.

If this is our destiny, how in the world are we going to become one with Christ? It's not going to be an Eastern religious experience where spirits just meld together and become one big spiritual nebula. The answer lies in the work of the Holy Spirit. He was always there in the Old Testament, just below the surface of everything that God did with his people. What nobody knew was how integral the Holy Spirit would be to our salvation. There is nothing in the Old Testament that teaches us that the Spirit of Christ is going to enter our spirits and make us one with Christ: this is strictly a New Testament theme. Jesus lives in us through his Spirit, and we live in him.

This is the mystery that the Apostles revealed to the Church.

I have been crucified with Christ and *I no longer live, but Christ lives in me*. The life I live in the body, I live by faith in the Son of God, who loved me and gave himself for me. (Galatians 2:20)

I have become its servant by the commission God gave me to present to you the word of God in its fullness – the *mystery* that has been kept hidden for ages and generations, but is now disclosed to the saints. To them God has chosen to make known among the Gentiles the glorious riches of this mystery, which is *Christ in you*, the hope of glory. (Colossians 1:25-27)

Jesus longed for the day when he could bring his "sheep" together and they would have fellowship with himself and with the Father – by becoming one with him.

I pray also for those who will believe in me through their message, that all of them may be one, Father, just as you are in me and I am in you. May they also be in us so that the world may believe that you have sent me. I have given them the glory that you gave me, that they may be one as we are one: I in them and you in me. May they be brought to complete unity to let the world know that you sent me and have loved them even as you have loved me. (John 17:20-23)

The act of making us one with Christ is a mystery indeed; nobody can understand how it works or how to make it happen. (See John 3:8 on this.) But the Creator who made the world knows how to recreate us in his image – a second Creation, not able to fall into sin and death again, but able to live in the presence of God forever. Making the Son of God a man was the open door for humanity to live with God. The way that you and I can take advantage of this new opportunity is to become one with Christ, the righteous Man, through the Spirit.

If you think that these are difficult concepts to grasp, you're right. Even the angels long to look into these things! Since God knew we would need help understanding the mystery of the Gospel, he gave us Apostles to explain it to us. You will also notice that they didn't spend much time on the basics; they were too busy explaining the new material, which is difficult enough to understand. They assumed that the reader has done his homework already in the Old Testament.

> We have much to say about this, but it is hard to explain because you are slow to learn. In fact, though by this time you ought to be teachers, you need someone to teach you the elementary truths of God's Word all over again. You need milk, not solid food! Anyone who lives on milk, being still an infant, is not acquainted with the teaching about righteousness. But solid food is for the mature, who by constant use have trained themselves to distinguish good from evil.
> Therefore let us leave the elementary teachings about Christ and go on to maturity, not laying again the foundation of repentance from acts that lead to death, and of faith in God, instruction about baptisms, the laying on of hands, the resurrection of the dead, and eternal judgment. And God permitting, we will do so. (Hebrews 5:11 – 6:3)

The disciples of Jesus (who were later the Apostles – the "ones sent out") were hand-picked eyewitnesses who spent three years with Jesus. They saw his works, they listened to his lessons, they pondered over the events surrounding the life of Christ. But even they had little idea of what was happening … until the Spirit of God filled them at Pentecost. Then the mystery was made plain to them and they had the supernatural ability to carry the *right* message to the nations. They saw the truth about *the nature of Christ* and they knew the steps that one should take *to become one with the Son of God*. The data was the same as before; but now they became the teachers of the Church. We understand the true nature of Christ and his work through their teachings.

> Consequently, you are no longer foreigners and aliens, but fellow citizens with God's people and members of God's household, *built on the foundation of the Apostles and Prophets*, with Christ Jesus himself as the chief cornerstone. (Ephesians 2:19-20)

Since the Spirit of Christ is the key to being one with Christ, the Apostles explain difficult but critical concepts like being filled with the Spirit, walking in the Spirit, not grieving the Spirit, and bearing spiritual fruit.

They also teach us a great deal about the New Creation. They don't want us to make the same mistake that the Jews made, thinking that the old physical system is God's ultimate goal for his people. The Epistles of the New Testament contrast the old world with the new world. They show us Heaven, and the glory of God in the Church. They press upon us the need for conversion of the soul, not just outward conformity to the Law. Of course, all this was taught in the Old Testament; but now the time had come to cut the cord with the physical and implement the spiritual Kingdom.

Speaking of the Jews, one point that the Apostles were careful to make clear is that anybody can come to Christ for salvation and the New Creation – it's not just for the Jews. The promise was always there in the Old Testament that God would eventually extend his plan around the world. The Jews were the first to learn about his Kingdom, but they are not the *only* ones allowed into God's Kingdom! It was always predicted that the Gentiles would eventually come into the family of God; the Old Testament, however, never fully explained how that was to happen. The reason for that is that it requires an understanding of the second mystery that the Apostles revealed to the world: that to become spiritual children of God, we must become one with Christ – not Jewish. In other words, it's not enough to be a Jew;

you must become a *Christian.* Both Jew and Gentile must do that to be a spiritual heir of Abraham.

> His purpose was to create in himself one new man out of the two, thus making peace … He came and preached peace to you who were far away and peace to those who were near. For through him we both have access to the Father by one Spirit. Consequently, you are no longer foreigners and aliens, but fellow citizens with God's people and members of God's household. (Ephesians 2:15, 17-19)

The Apostles were actually interpreters of Christ. Like the Pharisees, it was entirely possible to look at Jesus of Nazareth and miss the point about him. Because he came as a man, it was easy to miss his true glory. Only by faith can we see the Son of God in Jesus and his work. But just in case we missed the point in the Gospels from Jesus' teaching, the Apostles also focus on that point in their letters. There should be no mistaking their message: the Messiah has come to gather his people to himself and take them to Heaven. The old promises that God made to his people are true; but the *way* he plans to fulfill them is completely unexpected. This time it's going to work.

To summarize, the Old and New Testaments train you in how to carry out your Mission of preparing yourself to live with God. All the elements are there: the lessons given to the Israelites, and the lessons to Christians, will show you what works and what doesn't work. Man, with all his good intentions, could never rise high enough to please God. But then God always knew that; he had to prove that to us through the history of the Bible. We now have a failsafe way of reaching Heaven through his Son.

Using the Bible

Once you start to understand what is going on in the Bible, you will realize that *the Israelites were learning how to live with God.* This is the very thing that *we* want to learn! They first learned how to live in this world according to spiritual principles. Everything in the Old Testament system shows us how the reality of God affects us. The Creation, the Covenant, the Law, David's Kingdom, the Prophets – all these major themes reveal different aspects of God directing his people, rebuking them, saving them, ruling over them, leading them, protecting them, and blessing them. We actually do live in two worlds; we *have* to take God seriously.

So we have to study the Bible as if it's God's manual of life for his people, which it is. It covers all aspects of our life before God. It addresses all the problems that we will encounter in this world, and how to solve them. There is nothing missing that we are going to need.

This means that we can't ignore any of it. If we underline only the promises of God and ignore the rest of the Bible, we are opening ourselves up to dangerous situations for which we won't have any answers. As Paul told Timothy, *all* of Scripture is necessary for our spiritual survival – even those parts that are "unpleasant" to us.

> All Scripture is God-breathed and is useful for teaching, rebuking, correcting and training in righteousness, so that the man of God may be thoroughly equipped for every good work. (2 Timothy 3:16-17)

There are many parts of the Bible that the typical Christian ignores. We can't afford to do that, though, if we want to train for survival. For example, our biggest problem is <u>**sin**</u>. Sin is rebellion against God's rule over us. Obedience to God is what life is all about, and we have *not* been obeying him. Unless we understand this concept, we can't possibly be saved from our sin. Yet we almost never want to examine ourselves using God's standard of righteousness! When God purges us through hardship, he is targeting our sin; what will we do if we live in denial? How long will he have to punish us before we wake up to his urgent message – *to change now*?

If you want a good place to start working on this subject, study the Law and the Prophets. The *Law* is the statement of what *God* says is right and wrong. His standard judges us; we dare not use any other standard on ourselves. You will find the Law extremely uncomfortable as it probes your heart and mind, and roots out what God calls sin. Just remember that this is medicine for your soul, and master it. This is God's definition of a Perfect Man. You'll never measure up, but at the very least you will appreciate what Jesus has done for you and quit trying to do it yourself.

Another vital part of the Bible to study is the ***Prophets***. Here God confronts his people with their sin in no uncertain terms. Man is so clever at hiding his sin from others, and even from himself. But he can't hide anything from God. It's a healthy exercise to come into God's presence and let him examine us, take us apart and judge us, and tell us exactly what he sees in our hearts. Most people aren't going to like the experience of reading the Prophets. Yet it's a necessary first step to identifying exactly what's wrong in our hearts, minds and lives, so that we can move to the second step of actually dealing with that sin. Reading the Prophets is like experiencing Judgment Day ahead of time. Better now than later!

Once the Law and the Prophets convince us that we are sinners (which is the whole point of this exercise – it takes a good deal of humbling and convincing to get us to admit it!), we can take appropriate measures to crucify that sin using the means that God has provided for us. It's one thing to know that you are sick; it's quite another thing to take the right medicine to be healed. Though the world has its own answers to the problems of life, we Christians know from the Bible (Old *and* New Testaments) what we need – the spiritual medicine of Christ. Only in him will we have life. The New Testament helps us here.

Here's another subject that we have so much trouble with, yet the Bible is very clear about: the **church**. When it comes to the church, we all like to do it our own way; we have our own ideas of what church should be like. You know there's something wrong when there are a million variations of "church" in our world today! The Bible has a tremendous amount to teach us about church, and it's not all in the New Testament. For example, David was a man "after God's own heart," and he put together a nation before God that would satisfy all of God's plans for his people. That system that David incorporated in Israel is the model for today's church. Jesus, who was known as the Son of David, uses that same Davidic model as he puts together a vital church that accomplishes the Mission that God has for it. If we can see that, if we can connect the whole picture, all of our churches will become the

Church universal as God intended it to be. We will all be brothers and sisters in Christ –

> … so that the body of Christ may be built up until we all reach unity in the faith and in the knowledge of the Son of God and become mature, attaining to the whole measure of the fullness of Christ. (Ephesians 4:12-13)

The key, again, is using the Bible for what God designed it for: a blueprint for the Temple on earth. We are one Body, and we prove that we truly understand the Bible when we act like it.

Remember, *everything* in the Old and New Testaments teaches us how to live with God. You just have to bring it all together.

Bible study aids

To a brand-new Christian, it may seem an overwhelming task to learn the Bible to this extent! Many saints have had to do this on their own, and they've spent years "reinventing the wheel" as they struggled to put the whole picture of the Bible together to make a useable system.

But by God's wisdom there are teachers and preachers in the church who have done a lot of that work already. They are charged to teach and instruct the sheep with the wisdom that God has given them. Certainly every saint has the Spirit of revelation, and they all have Bibles – so they *could* learn it on their own. Life, however, often won't wait. Problems come up at any time, and we need answers now. The church leaders can help accelerate your learning process if you're not too proud to learn from them.

There are also good Bible study books available to help you get a grasp on the Bible's message and main themes. Just be careful here, because there are also *a lot* of books that are no good. Jesus warned us that there would be wolves among the sheep, and in our day those wolves are doing their best to talk us out of taking the Bible seriously. The Liberals are actually unbelievers in Christian dress. If you find any book or teacher who tells you that you don't have to take the Bible at face value, or that it's not your ultimate authority, or that it's a work of man instead of God – throw that book away.

A good measure for a Bible study book is this: does it teach you about the God of the Bible? Remember that the Bible reveals God to us; a book that claims to make the Bible clear to us will be doing the same thing. And be careful of books that are actually no more than works on psychology or sociology. **Man**-centered religion focuses completely on our "good behavior," or ways of living that we think are right and proper. **God**-centered religion starts with studying God; our behavior will be made plain as we study him first.

Here is a list of books available from Ravenbrook Publishers and what you can learn from them:

Mystery Revealed: A Beginner's Bible Survey

This book covers the background of the Bible's history, the message of the whole Bible, and then takes the student through each section of the Bible to see how the important stories fit into the overall picture or message of the Bible.

Eight Fundamentals of the Christian Faith

According to Hebrews 5, there are certain foundations of our faith that every Christian ought to know well. This book examines those foundations that the passage in Hebrews mentions.

The Throne of David

David put the nation of Israel together according to God's plan – five principles that made the Israelites a strong nation under God. He gave Israel a Mission that was clear and attainable. Jesus puts his church together according to that same plan.

Ten Keys to the Bible

In order to understand what the Bible teaches, there are ten principles that the student can learn which will "unlock" any passage in the Bible and give its clear meaning.

The Witness

The Bible is actually a collection of affidavits of eyewitnesses of God who can testify of his reality and how he works. This book shows how God put the Bible together from these eyewitness accounts so that there can be no successful argument against it.

The Bible Explains Creation

Genesis is not the only passage in the Bible that explains how Creation happened. By using teachings from the entire Bible, we can better understand what happened at Creation. The subject is much bigger than people think; God laid down spiritual foundations at Creation that guide and control our physical world.

The Secret to Answered Prayer

If you want answers to your prayers, you have to learn how to approach God in the way that he expects of you. He won't listen to someone with the wrong attitude! Six principles will get you in the right frame of heart for finding God.

There are many other books available that will help you learn the Bible. If you need help finding them, ask someone you can trust for more help.

How much do we need to know?

It may sound as if we are encouraging people to become nothing less than experts in the Bible! Just how much is the ordinary church member supposed to learn? How will he or she know that they have learned what they *need* to know? What difference is there between the pastor and the layman?

For one thing, there should be less difference between the pastor and layman than you may think. So many people expect the pastor to know all about the Bible, while they sit back and swallow little bits of what he has already chewed for them! After all, don't they pay the pastor to be the expert? But the solution to this is best explained by using a military example. The sergeant is paid to train the recruits. Out in the battlefield, however, the recruits do the fighting – not just the sergeant! Paul told Timothy that the purpose of the Bible, and those in the church who are paid to teach it, is to *train* the members to do the work. In other words, *you* are to be the expert here. If you don't understand that, then you are going to die on the battlefield.

You are going to be facing all sorts of problems, trials, crises, disasters, confusing situations, battles, and failures in the years ahead. What are you going to do? You can't pay the pastor to solve them for you! You will have to know the right road to take, the right words to say, the right actions to follow.

There will be times when the situation you're in will be confusing; you won't understand what's going on. Could it be that God is working behind the scenes and you didn't realize it? Could it be that you don't know how God works, that you don't know the way he likes to go about things? Could it be that you not only don't know his ways, you don't like the way he does things? If so, you won't be any better off than the Israelites who also didn't know his ways.

> That is why I was angry with that generation, and I said, 'Their hearts are always going astray, and they have not known my ways.' So I declared on oath in my anger, 'They shall never enter my rest.' (Hebrews 3:10-11)

You may stumble over the simplest problems in life simply because you failed to learn the right lesson from the Bible. The book of Proverbs gives us wonderful principles to use for all sorts of situations that the ordinary person meets in everyday life. Which ones have you mastered so far? Will you be able to recall the right response in the middle of the crisis? Do you know all the appropriate responses to anger, to the works of the wicked, to fools, to laziness, to adultery? As Proverbs itself tells us, the wise will spend a lot of time learning *ahead of time* the kinds of things that they will need in future trials.

> The proverbs of Solomon son of David, king of Israel: for attaining wisdom and discipline; for understanding words of insight; for acquiring a disciplined and prudent life, doing what is right and just and fair; for giving prudence to the simple, knowledge and discretion to the young – let the wise listen and add to their learning, and let the discerning get guidance – for understanding proverbs and parables, the sayings and riddles of the wise. (Proverbs 1:1-6)

Conversion is the first crucial step toward God. We must be saved from our sin and be made alive to God if we hope to live in eternity. Do you know whether this has really happened to you? Genesis describes the basic elements of the "new creation." The story of Abraham lays out the Gospel in clear terms, and what it takes to inherit those promises in Christ. The Law tells us what we are saved from – our sin, and where God is taking us – his righteousness. The Prophets know how to examine our hearts and see if we really are converted. The Apostles aren't fooled by false converts, because they know what makes the difference between a weed that eventually dies off and the wheat that is firmly rooted in life: union with Christ. As you can see, everywhere you look in the Bible, you will find information about what a true conversion is. Now – using this information, did God truly convert you, or are you simply calling yourself a Christian without his power backing up that claim?

Fortunately God does the important work in us so that, for example, we don't have to worry if the Spirit is really in our hearts – if he saved us. God gives us spiritual life in the same way that we were given breath when we were born. Yet while he does his part, we are responsible to learn and mature in order to work in his spiritual world. Remember that it took you many years to get through school! What you did with that education explains where you are now in life. And what you do with the Bible will affect your *spiritual* standing in God's Kingdom. Learn and survive.

Dealing with the Enemy

The difference between success and failure, survival and defeat, depends on whether you can see what's really going on around you. Confusion will paralyze you; not being able to understand what's happening to you, you will sit in the dust like Job and blame God and man for the trials that you are going through.

The Enemy loves it when you are in confusion.

One of the most important survival skills for a Christian is to be able to see that he's in the middle of a war. A great deal is at stake here, not least the eternal state of your soul. It's time to wake up to reality and arm yourself against the Enemy.

War

In every war there are two parties: the one who started the trouble, and the one who is defending himself. Usually the one who starts the war is the culprit, and though he might justify his actions in his own mind, it's not so easy to convince his neighbors of his good intentions in light of all the trouble he is causing. His victim occupies the moral high ground; everyone understands that he has a right to defend himself against aggression.

It may come as a surprise to you, but you are *surrounded* by enemies. Like it or not, Christian, you are in the middle of a war. Your enemies are bringing the conflict right to your doorstep. Fortunately you are on the high ground; you can defeat them if you know what you're doing.

The first step in any conflict is to ***identify the enemy***. We have to know, *first*, who exactly is trying to destroy us, and *second*, we have to be willing to call them the enemy. The first step is crucial for every believer; people are just too willing to fight the wrong enemy – usually

97

each other! The second step – the willingness to fight – comes hard for those who love peace. If we don't admit that we are at war, and take steps to deal with the enemy, we will most certainly be destroyed.

So, who are these enemies who are out to destroy us?

- ***The world*** – We already looked at the fact that the world is not our friend. The "world" that man has created is *not* what God first created! It is filled with specially designed pitfalls that will appeal to our lusts; this world is a playground for the wicked, for anybody who wants to follow roads away from God, and into self-glory and fulfilling one's lusts.

- ***The flesh*** – *The sinful mind is hostile to God. It does not submit to God's Law, nor can it do so. Those controlled by the sinful nature cannot please God.* (Romans 8:5-8) As if we needed more trouble, our very natures are to blame for the trouble we get into. We can't just blame the world, our parents, our genetic makeup, or the devil; we sin because we *want* to. As Eve discovered in the Garden, the temptation appeals to our desires; so, using our desires as the standard, we take action on the temptation.

- ***The devil*** – *The devil … was a murderer from the beginning, not holding to the truth, for there is no truth in him. When he lies, he speaks his native language, for he is a liar and the father of lies.* (John 8:44) The plot thickens, as most stories do, with the introduction of the arch-villain. Not that we can blame him for our sins; we are still guilty and fully responsible. But it sure doesn't help matters that we have such a formidable and ruthless opponent who is determined to destroy us – and he knows all too well how to do that. The devil is a master of lies and deceit. Satan's main method is to lie to us, to deceive us and get us to believe anything other than the truth of God. Then we willingly walk into a trap and get destroyed.

Once you've identified the enemy, you can move to the next step – which is to ***identify what they are doing to you***. These enemies have a definite objective in mind. But in time of war, the enemy will never let you in on what their objectives are. That would give away their secrets! If you knew what they were doing, there wouldn't be any surprise in their attack and you might mount an effective defense against them. Therefore, so that you aren't in the dark about what's going on, your goal is to "know your enemy."

We have powerful resources on our side for understanding the nature of the enemy's attack on us. God sits above the world, and nobody has any secrets from him. He sees the hearts of all men.

> For the Word of God is living and active. Sharper than any double-edged sword, it penetrates even to dividing soul and spirit, joints and marrow; it judges the thoughts and attitudes of the heart. Nothing in all creation is hidden from God's sight. Everything is uncovered and laid bare before the eyes of him to whom we must give account. (Hebrews 4:12-13)

The Word of God is how we know the strategy of Satan – that he lies and contradicts the Bible. Through the Word we know what it is about the world that makes it so dangerous. The Word shows us the hearts of men and what they are up to. Without the Bible, we are confused about everything; armed with the Bible, we "walk in the light" while our enemies are confused.

The third step is to **put together a strategy of war**. You know, as a Christian, where you want to go – to be with God. Now that you've done your homework on the enemy, you know exactly what they are doing to prevent you from reaching that objective. All you have to do now is develop an effective strategy of your own to defend yourself against the enemy's attacks, and find the right weapons that will push them back in defeat. You must not let your enemies stop you in your Mission.

Willing to fight

Most people are like sheep. They don't like to fight. And in a relatively peaceful society like ours, there's no need to fight – just go to work, raise the family, take vacations, and enjoy life.

But as the saying goes, sometimes the fight comes to you, and you can't avoid it.

You don't have any choice about this war. As soon as you took upon yourself the name of Christ, you became an instant target for your enemies.

> All men will hate you because of me, but he who stands firm to the end will be saved. (Matthew 10:22)

We may be tempted to give up, because the problems of life seem so overwhelming. So often we are completely alone in our battles and we can't find any solutions. But there's no reason to give up; God has given us everything, including the victory. As long as Jesus lives and reigns in Heaven, we are assured of complete victory.

> If God is for us, who can be against us? ... Who will bring any charge against those whom God has chosen? It is God who justifies. Who is he that condemns? Christ Jesus, who died – more than that, who was raised to life – is at the right hand of God and is also interceding for us. Who shall separate us from the love of Christ? Shall trouble or hardship or persecution or famine or nakedness or danger or sword? ... No, in all these things we are more than conquerors through him who loved us. For I am convinced that neither death nor life, neither angels nor demons, neither the present nor the future, nor any powers, neither height nor depth, nor anything else in all creation, will be able to separate us from the love of God that is in Christ Jesus our Lord. (Romans 8:31, 33-35, 38-39)

Notice that he lists all sorts of hardships and trials. We may think that we would never survive such trials; but the only ones who will fail in the end are those without faith in Christ. If someone shies away from a confrontation with the enemy because "they don't like to fight," they will be branded cowards – and God particularly despises cowards.

> But the *cowardly*, the unbelieving, the vile, the murderers, the sexually immoral, those who practice magic arts, the idolaters and all liars – their place will be in the fiery lake of burning sulfur. This is the second death. (Revelation 21:8)

The Mission

Every army has a mission to accomplish. They spend a lot of time training for all kinds of missions, but the commanders know the specific mission that they are training for. They have a specific enemy to conquer, a territory to overrun, a dictator to bring down. When they take their army to the field, they will do everything they can to achieve that mission before they bring the army back home.

The church has a Mission too; and, like a military mission, ours is also clear and attainable. The church's Mission is twofold:

- **First**, we have to be thoroughly delivered of our sins – our immorality, our waywardness, our ignorance, our willfulness, our rebellion, our lawlessness, our independent attitude. The job of the Christian is to come back to God, humble himself, submit to his rule, and serve him. We have to *change*, from sinner to saint. The ministry of the church *has* to address that need.

- **Second**, we have to start getting used to the new world that Jesus is preparing for us. We have to put our minds on things above, learn God's ways, live in the righteousness of Christ, start frequenting the Temple in Heaven, wean ourselves away from this physical world and start storing up treasures in Heaven, learn to be holy and set apart for God's use.

There's a lot to be done in these two areas. It's surprising that so many people are doing hardly anything to address these key issues and yet they still have hopes of Heaven someday. It will take all the resources of a church's ministry to successfully prepare its members for this kind of life. I know, it's not much fun to focus on your sin when you go to church. It's like finding out that we have cancer, or going through a heart attack. It's not exactly what we were planning to do with our free time! This problem has been forced upon us, however, and now we have to deal with it or die. *The Bible's entire message revolves around this issue of what is going to be done about our sin.*

People naturally want the church to address other problems in their lives – family problems, job problems, neighbor problems, financial problems, health problems.   But Christians have to understand that these, though important, are *not* the primary Mission of the church. These other issues will be addressed, even some of them solved, *only if people focus on the two main issues of our faith.*   If we make real progress on the primary Mission, that will start straightening out other problems along the way.   This is the teaching of God's Word.

Principles of war

There ought to be classes in church about how to fight against our enemies.   So little is being done in this area, which is why so many people are suffering at the enemy's hands.   A mob without discipline and training will always suffer defeat before a determined foe.

The army trains its soldiers for a good reason: their survival, and accomplishing the Mission, is at stake.   It takes months and years to turn a well-meaning but helpless civilian into a trained warrior.   In fact, most young men going into the military aren't aware at all of what is about to happen to them; they only *thought* they were ready to fight! The drill sergeants are going to hit them with a lifestyle that they little imagined in civilian life.   They are going to *change.*

It should be the same way in the church, but sadly it isn't.   Helpless "civilians" remain helpless; they have no idea why trouble comes upon them, or what to do when it does.   The enemy is having a field day in our modern churches because nobody is prepared to defend themselves against him.   It's like a country without an army.

The shame is that it isn't difficult to get trained and ready to fight our spiritual battles.   Anybody can understand the principles involved, and all it takes is discipline and determination (and love for the cause!) to become an effective Christian soldier.   Here are some of the more important principles of warfare.

Stay in touch with your resources.   In other words, keep the way open and clear between you and God.   *He* is your source of strength, wisdom, and purpose.   The treasures of Heaven, and the spiritual weapons that come from God's armory, are your only hope for survival.

Keeping that supply line open to God is vitally important. Napoleon said once that any general who gets cut off from his supply line ought to be shot. In other words, *whatever* you do, don't lose touch with your resources. Your supply line is your *life*; you get food, weapons and orders from there; it's your retreat in tough times. From there the Lord will send firepower to your position when you call for it. Whatever you do, wherever you go, it's crucial for you to keep in touch with God at all times.

So many people aren't careful about this, and then they wonder why they get trapped by the enemy with no escape, no hope, and they get destroyed. Prayer doesn't help, the Bible doesn't help, they get no help from others – and down they go in despair.

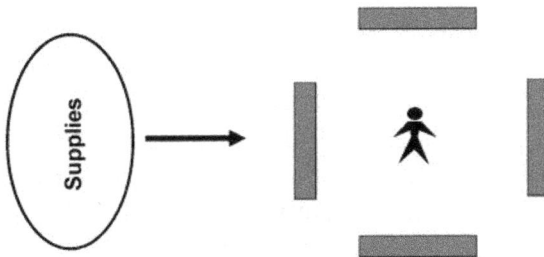

Cut off from help

As you can see from this picture, this person let the enemy surround him, and now he can't get back to safety. Whatever he does will end in defeat. It didn't need to end that way! The Lord warns us over and over to stay in touch with him.

Pray continually. (1 Thessalonians 5:17)

One thing I ask of the LORD, this is what I seek: that I may dwell in the house of the LORD all the days of my life, to gaze upon the beauty of the LORD and to seek him in his temple. For in the day of trouble he will keep me safe in his dwelling; he will hide me in the shelter of his tabernacle and set me high upon a rock. Then my head will be exalted above the enemies who surround me; at his tabernacle will I sacrifice with shouts of joy; I will sing and make music to the LORD. (Psalm 27:4-6)

The key to staying in touch with God is, as we've seen already, personal holiness. You have to be and stay God-centered at all times. Stay in his Word; "His delight is in the Law of the LORD, and on his Law he meditates day and night." (Psalm 1:2) Immerse yourself in his Word, learn about every aspect of God, long for God's spiritual treasures. The more time you spend in the Halls of Heaven through the Bible, the stronger your connection with God will be, and the enemy won't be able to hurt you.

Follow the Spirit in whatever way he leads you – which is always going to be toward God, not away from him. As the Spirit works with you, he will cleanse you of the sin and moral filth that still stain your heart and mind to make you acceptable to God. The Spirit will illuminate the world of God for you in the Bible, and lead you to the throne of God to taste and enjoy the treasures of Heaven. That's why Paul said to follow the leading of the Spirit.

So I say, live by the Spirit, and you will not gratify the desires of the sinful nature ... Since we live by the Spirit, let us keep in step with the Spirit. (Galatians 5:16, 25)

And pray in the Spirit on all occasions with all kinds of prayers and requests. (Ephesians 6:18)

One way to keep that supply line intact is not to run ahead of God. As he leads you in life, follow his orders and do exactly what he tells you. So many people in their zeal and ignorance run out on their own, determined to do their own thing and get what they want in life, not worrying at all about whether God is behind it; all they want from him is his blessing. Then they find themselves alone and surrounded, in trouble and with no answers, because they were doing something that God didn't want them to do. They were no longer walking with God. The Bible says for good reason that we have to learn to *wait on the Lord*. He is the center of the army; we support him, and serve him – not the other way around. A good general will go out with his troops; and a good soldier, if he has any sense at all, will stay close to his general. If we don't know what the next step is, then we should stop and wait on him to give us our orders.

How many churches have made this fatal error! Without checking with the Lord of the church to see what *he* wants done, everyone charges off in zeal (and ignorance) to fill their churches with what they think ought to be there. The preachers teach on whatever subject strikes their fancy (or, what is worse, what they think the people want to hear). The church members beg and insist on programs and functions that have nothing to do with the Mission. Everyone is happy when their church is filled with things they like, and everyone complains when the church doesn't suit them.

Only the wise, however, go back to the Lord and learn about the Mission. Church functions are designed in such a way that the people are saved from their sins (their *actual* sins; this is not just an academic concept – we want to see people changing from nasty to nice!). Leaders put together the church program in such a way that the members are learning how to live in God's spiritual world, and they are cutting ties with this world. They refuse to allow extra programs and functions that don't relate to the Mission; why waste time and resources on things that the church has no business doing?

You see, there are two roads to take: either take your own road without God, or take his road and walk with him. Only when you follow him will you be assured of success. Moses understood this very well.

> The LORD replied, "My Presence will go with you, and I will give you rest." Then Moses said to

him, "If your Presence does not go with us, do not send us up from here. How will anyone know that you are pleased with me and with your people unless you go with us?" (Exodus 33:14-16)

One more important point about maintaining your supply line. One of the ways that God likes to do things is to use man to do his work. He rarely comes down and works miracles out of the blue when he's supplying his people; he uses your brothers and sisters in the church to supply your needs. *You need to recognize this* – your church is a vital road for the supply line back to God. When they are doing *their* job, you will receive the spiritual food and resources that you need to do *your* job in God's Kingdom. Here is where the gifts of the Spirit come in. The army of God is *not* a one-man-show. We need each other; it's a team effort. We can't defeat the enemy by ourselves, nor does God send us out alone to do that job. The power and wisdom of God is distributed among the people of God; the body of Christ is made up of many members with different gifts and abilities. Each has their role, their function, in the body, and we need each other. Just remember the military maxim: *divide and conquer*. If you are separated from the church, you are easily destroyed, because a loner doesn't have the necessary resources to survive. The church is a vital avenue to your supply in Heaven.

Understand the authority structure. Probably the next most difficult problem that the military has to solve is the self-will and independence deep inside all of us. Recruits *have* to learn the hierarchy above them. The military runs by authority and command; it can't possibly achieve its objectives if every man is doing his own thing.

Many in the church in our day, however, have largely lost this respect for authority. Everyone is doing his own thing. People don't mind having a leader, though; in fact, they like to have the leader up front – so that they can pick on him, work him to death, blame him for their problems, and so on.

Probably the main difference between the military and the church is that the military trains its recruits, and the church isn't in training mode at all – it's in entertainment mode. In the army, you *have* to do what the sergeant tells you to do. He's giving you skills that you will need in battle. Everyone knows that. But in the church, members primarily are looking for someone to please them, coddle them and give them what they want. They don't see the pastor or elder as an authority that they have to follow to be trained in their faith. We hired those "leaders," and now they have to measure up to the congregation's expectations. They had better please and entertain us or they will be fired.

So the sergeant is respected and obeyed, and the pastor is used and abused. The sergeant is the leader and authority, and the pastor is an employee.

We're not going to get any training done with an attitude like that. Christian leaders aren't supposed to be abusive like a drill sergeant often is, but their job *is* the same: to train and equip the members of the church, to hone and sharpen their skills, and send them out to accomplish the Mission.

The church is a big family, and like any family its members are at different spiritual levels. Some are mature and experienced; some are infants who simply can't take care of themselves; and the rest are found at various levels of maturity. Hardly anybody is at the same level! But that's all right; there's nothing wrong with being immature – at the beginning. The problem is if we *stay* immature, in spite of the church's best efforts at getting us to grow.

The elders in a church are chosen because they have more Christian maturity, they have spiritual skills, and they have the experience of battle that the rest of the church needs. These leaders are called by God to their position to train the rest of us.

> It was he who gave some to be Apostles, some to be Prophets, some to be evangelists, and some to be pastors and teachers, to prepare God's people for

works of service, so that the body of Christ may be built up until we all reach unity in the faith and in the knowledge of the Son of God and become mature, attaining to the whole measure of the fullness of Christ. Then we will no longer be infants, tossed back and forth by the waves, and blown here and there by every wind of teaching and by the cunning and craftiness of men in their deceitful scheming. Instead, speaking the truth in love, we will in all things grow up into him who is the Head, that is, Christ. (Ephesians 4:11-15)

Notice that *Christ* appointed these leaders for the benefit of the church. They get their authority from *him*, not from the congregation. They are answerable to *him*, not the church. (1 Peter 5:1-4) The church *has* to understand this principle of leadership and submit to their ministry. When they rebel against their leaders, they are rebelling against the Lord who appointed them.

Obey your leaders and submit to their authority. They keep watch over you as men who must give an account. Obey them so that their work will be a joy, not a burden, for that would be of no advantage to you. (Hebrews 13:17)

Organization is the first order of business in any new endeavor. Someone has to be in charge, and he appoints other leaders under him to carry out his orders. Not everyone is going to be a leader! You've heard the saying, "all chiefs and no Indians!" You need troops, and lots of them, to fight a battle; and you need a few officers to train, organize, and direct the troops. Some private in the ranks may *want* to be a general; he may think that he *ought* to be a general; but until he's actually made a general, he had better stay in the ranks and do his duty or he will mess everything up royally.

The extreme democratic spirit in our churches today is crippling the church's ability to fight. Almost nobody is willing to submit to authority in the church. But people don't understand the situation here. Jesus wants us to win, not to lose; so, he organized the church for discipline and training. He specially appointed leaders in the church to help us achieve our objectives. They are not there to hurt you (the good ones!); they are there to train you to fight the enemy. Submit to their authority, learn from their ministry. If you don't submit, your church probably won't have the backbone to rebuke you for your rebellion, but you can be sure that you will have to answer to the Lord for your rebellious spirit. Deserters and rebels will be severely disciplined.

The leaders also have to stop living in fear. Ministry is not a popularity contest. They are not called to work in a way that will "please the people," but in a way that will please the Master. This requires exercising authority in the church – not to "lord it over" poor church members, but to organize and direct the troops efficiently against the enemy.

Get yourself ready! Stand up and say to them whatever I command you. Do not be terrified by them, or I will terrify you before them. (Jeremiah 1:17)

These, then, are the things you should teach. Encourage and rebuke with all authority. Do not let anyone despise you. (Titus 2:15)

Be shepherds of God's flock that is under your care, serving as overseers – not because you must, but because you are willing, as God wants you to be; not greedy for money, but eager to serve; not lording it over those entrusted to you, but being examples to the flock. (1 Peter 5:2-3)

It's true that you won't make many friends when you do your duty, but then hardly anybody *likes* the drill sergeant! He isn't doing his job to be liked; he's saving your life by relentlessly drilling life-saving skills into your mind and body.

There's a reason why church leaders are called "elders" – they are older and wiser, they're more experienced in the things of God, they've been walking with God for years, and they know what you will need better than you do. The wise – or those who want to be wise – will sit at their feet and learn.

Will there be problems? Of course; we are all human, and leaders are sinners just as other people are. But there are two things to remember here: *first*, those who have problems with the leaders had better look to themselves first. *Accusations against leaders are usually from discontented, ignorant rebels who don't know what they're talking about.* Leaders have a lot that they're responsible for; they know a lot more about a given situation than you do; and they are skilled at their job – after all, that's why they are leaders. But because they are leaders and always in the public eye, they are natural targets for the ignorant. That's why there's a safeguard in Scripture for accusing elders of wrongdoing; following this will eliminate 95% of the false charges brought against them.

> Do not entertain an accusation against an elder unless it is brought by two or three witnesses. (1 Timothy 5:19)

Second, the church leader is Christ's employee, an under-shepherd of sorts. He is to do only what Christ tells him to do. He himself is in training; he has to live out the same principles that he is teaching you.

> Follow my example, as I follow the example of Christ. (1 Corinthians 11:1)

What are Christ's commands? You can easily look them up for yourself in the Bible; there are no secrets here. If your leader is living the kind of life that the Bible requires, then follow that person – he's following his Master and you want to go with him. Of course if he isn't living as the Bible says to live, that will be plain to see also, and the church needs to deal with it. But the standard is always the Bible, the revealed will of God – never the whims of the congregation or the pride and power-lust of a ruthless tyrant.

Drill, drill, drill! The secret to successful warfare is *preparation* and *training*.

War requires a lot of training, memorization, studying, and practice. Yet there is almost none of this in today's churches. Sermons are like shotgun pellets – lots of points, scattering all over the place, almost nothing hitting the target. Nobody is required to train at anything or learn anything. There's no homework to do, no tests to take, there's no way of knowing whether anything is getting through. Ministries almost compete with each other at making church easier, less demanding, and more "fun" for the entire family.

I know it's the current practice for churches to focus on the love of God, and celebrating, and lots of touchy-feely issues that satisfy the effeminate. But study the Bible for a while with war in mind. You will find that God is training us for battle; he wants us to be realistic about what is about to happen.

There's no such thing as being too religious! The world considers us fanatics for taking our religion seriously. Well, you could call the soldier in the army a fanatic for the same reason: he's training for war, and the civilian isn't. When the enemy comes, the civilian will run and hide while the soldier will stand and fight. *That's* the difference.

Psalm 1 tells us that the man of God *meditates* on God's Law *day and night*. Jesus told us that we must be *perfect*, even as the Father in Heaven is perfect. We take orders from God, not man; therefore we have to measure up to God's standards, not man's. God expects much more from you than man ever could!

In sports, athletes set the bar higher and higher as they train, so that they can get better at their skills. The lazy, however, like to set the bar lower and lower so that it gets easier for them and they don't have to expend so much effort. Unfortunately very few people in the church are setting the bar higher. They insist on a religion that makes as few demands on them as possible, so that they have time and energy for the things of the world. That will *not* get them ready for the trials of life.

The Bible says that we need to become *experts* in our religion.

> In fact, though by this time you ought to be teachers, you need someone to teach you the elementary truths of God's Word all over again. You need milk, not solid food! Anyone who lives on milk, being still an infant, is not acquainted with the teaching about righteousness. But solid food is for the mature, who by constant use have trained themselves to distinguish good from evil. (Hebrews 5:12-14)

Keep in mind that people everywhere are dying from their sins. The temptations of this world are tearing apart our entire civilization. The devil's lies fill the media, the educational institutions, the business world, the political arena; they dominate our culture's way of life. The enemy has no mercy. What is needed are determined and well-trained soldiers to fight this war, not well-intentioned but helpless civilians.

> My people are destroyed for lack of knowledge. (Hosea 4:6)

How does one train in Christianity? Paul tells Timothy to start with the Word.

> All Scripture is God-breathed and is useful for teaching, rebuking, correcting and training in

righteousness, so that the man of God may be thoroughly equipped for every good work. (2 Timothy 3:16-17)

Notice that he *starts* with Scripture. This is the foundation of all discipline; otherwise what will happen in a church is only the work of man. Churches become little kingdoms where men appropriate the glory and authority due to Christ alone and force the members to do their bidding. It's true that men must carry out the work of discipline in the church, but we know that it will be *Christ's* kingdom when they carefully follow the instructions in Christ's Word. God will honor his Word, and he will give success to those who build his Kingdom using his materials. "For no one can lay any foundation other than the one already laid, which is Jesus Christ." (1 Corinthians 3:11)

The Bible is specially designed to do four things for us.

__Teaching__ – This takes many forms in the church. The obvious ones are the preaching and teaching that the church leaders do every Sunday. But there are other settings where teaching is going on. For example, the older women are told to instruct the younger women, parents are told to instruct their children, and elders are to lead young men by example.

The importance of teaching is based on the fact that we are learning creatures. Our heads are the first target of truth; through our eyes and ears, we take in information and process it in our brains. Our minds have to grasp the truth first, since the mind is the seat of all that we do and say.

Do not conform any longer to the pattern of this world, but be transformed by the *renewing of your mind*. Then you will be able to test and approve what God's will is – his good, pleasing and perfect will. (Romans 12:2)

From there the mind affects the heart with its emotions and feelings. In other words, truth guides our hearts – not the other way around.

How much teaching should go on in the church? Well, like a child growing up, we need to learn the basics first, which is what Hebrews 5:12 refers to. Then as we get older we learn more of what the world is like and how to make our way around in it. I guess it depends on what your aspirations are – if you're content to live on the bottom rung, with only a low-level job and barely getting along, twelve years of school should suffice. However, if you want to honor God with your entire life and do your utmost for him, it will take a lifetime to learn all about God and his Kingdom. There is no such thing as learning too much about this amazing new world that God has for his people.

__Rebuking__ – Oh that the modern church knew more of this blessing! "An honest answer is like a kiss on the lips." (Proverbs 24:26) People have an entirely wrong view of a rebuke. When given in love – and our brothers, including the elders, do it out of love for us – it is designed to help us. Instead, people get insulted and either lash back in anger or leave the church. What a pity.

This is no time for pride! The Mission of the church is to save us from our sin. If we don't believe that then perhaps we ought to save everyone else a lot of trouble and stay home! We are sinners; we are not perfect people, and we are not yet ready to live with God – not the way we are now. There is a lot of cleanup to be done in our hearts and lives. A true Christian who wants to be saved from sin will not back away from this truth, but rather will look eagerly for opportunities to address the problem.

It *is* the church's business to address your sin. People suffering from adult pride don't want anybody else meddling in their private lives. It's true that the elders shouldn't follow you home and put everything you do to a test; it's your business to clean your own face, spiritually, since you know best where you are dirty. It isn't true, though, that you are safe from having to face your sins in church. The sermons are going to address your sin, and your brothers will be offended by it; so, you must reach out and eagerly take the medicine for your soul offered to you in the ministry of the church if you hope to gain eternal life.

It's a spiritually healthy exercise to act like the tax collector when you're at church. He came humbly, ready to be talked to, admitting he was not pure but in great need of salvation. As Jesus said, *this* kind of person will go home from church accepted by God. He went there for the right thing, and he got it. (Luke 18:13-14)

How many church crises could we avoid if people were more open to being rebuked! We punish children when they don't listen to a rebuke to stop unacceptable behavior; we know that, if they'll simply listen and do what we say, the situation will get straightened out and we can go back to business. We don't hate them! It therefore frustrates us when they don't respond positively and change; getting mad at us only makes matters worse.

In the church, pride usually gets in the way and makes it impossible to work things out. *It's the mark of a true Christian to accept a rebuke when deserved* – and God makes it plain in his Word when we deserve it. If you turn away from that rebuke and leave, you lose. You may never get another chance at salvation if you despise God's Word and authority over you like that. It's the very definition of sin itself to reject the rebuke out of pride. So tread carefully.

He who listens to a life-giving rebuke will be at home among the wise. (Proverbs 15:31)

Correcting – This is the testing part of discipline and almost never done in today's churches. In schools the teachers will give the students a test to see how much they've learned in a subject. The test isn't designed to depress the students about what they couldn't remember. It's designed to point out to them the areas they still need help in. It's an examination of what they know compared to what they ought to know, what they really need to know, if they want to master the subject. It's that examination aspect that we don't do in church.

Let's use an example to illustrate this necessary feature of discipline. I've heard a lot of prayers from church members over the years. All kinds of prayers. Usually people pray whatever pops into their heads and hearts on the spur of the moment. It is, as one writer lamented once, the least practiced and least prepared-for part of worship.

But for all the fervency of these prayers, they rarely measured up to Biblical standards. The Bible tells us plainly how to approach God in prayer. It tells us what the agenda of prayer should be. It tells us when to pray. It shows us model prayers from experienced prayer warriors. And yet, even though the Bible is so specific about what prayer should be like, I've seen almost no attempt to apply those standards to the way people pray today in church. It's as if they don't want to be bothered with God's instructions on prayer! They often won't even bring a Bible to the prayer service!

People aren't testing what they are doing against the Word of God. I guess that pastors are so thankful when a person wants to do *anything* in the church that they are really reluctant to put their actions to the test.

But letting anything happen is fatal to the life of the church. Not just any sacrifice offered will do; we learn that from the Old Testament. Good intentions aren't enough – we have to live by the truth of God.

Aaron's sons were killed because they offered a sacrifice of their own design to God. Uzzah was struck dead because he violated the principles of how to approach God's holy altar. Saul was dethroned because he changed God's commands just a little bit to something more reasonable to him. God refused to listen to the Israelites' prayers because they still harbored sin in their hearts. The point is that we can't make up what we will do to please God. We have to do things in the way he specified – and that requires correcting our actions to fit his standards.

There is a true faith and a false faith; there are good works that please God and "good" works that don't please him; there is prayer that reaches his throne and prayer that doesn't; there is acceptable warfare against the enemy and unacceptable warfare; there are God's ways and man's ways. Now unless you're as wise as Jesus is, you're going to get a lot of this wrong before you get it right. Your willingness to be corrected will make the difference between success and failure.

> Examine yourselves to see whether you are in the faith; test yourselves. Do you not realize that Christ Jesus is in you – unless, of course, you fail the test? (2 Corinthians 13:5)

Training in righteousness – This too is almost never done in the church. Training is a long procedure of drills to get the material or exercise firmly embedded in the mind and instinct. The military, again, provides a useful model. The drill sergeant puts his poor recruits through endless drills day after day. After weeks and months of constant drills and

117

training the soldiers are thoroughly sick of training! The beauty of this training program is this – when they are actually in combat, in the middle of a situation that they trained for, the necessary actions are instinctive. They move quickly, efficiently, and effectively. They succeed. And it's all because of the thoroughness of the training.

The typical church almost never trains its people for anything. Sunday after Sunday they sit passively and listen to a sermon they often can't follow and almost never remember. They go to fellowship meals. They help out in fund drives. In fact, church has turned into having the most fun and expending the least effort – by design. Not only are they not training in spiritual matters, they don't even know why they are there!

The Mission of the church is to get us all out of our sins and living a righteous life. Though we are often told to do that, there is usually no training for it. Probably many church leaders wouldn't know where to start on this. How does one *train for righteousness*?

Faith is one of the spiritual abilities that the Holy Spirit gives us upon conversion. In fact, as we follow the Spirit – we dare not follow the Law itself! – we will learn how to live in this perfect righteousness of Christ. (See Paul's argument in Galatians 1-3.)

The point is that this requires a dedicated heart, a learning mind, the power of God, lots of opportunities, humility in the face of failure, thankfulness to God in success, and *time*. Training like this doesn't come easily or quickly.

Discipline happens best in the church. In fact, its only real chance of success is in the setting of the church. The resources and spiritual gifts are there, the personnel and experts in spiritual care are there, the opportunities are there.

So who in their right minds would pass up this opportunity to be saved to the uttermost?

Almost everyone, it seems! People aren't willing to admit their spiritual needs to others; they prefer to work on whatever shortcomings they think they may have on their own, at home, where nobody else will know about it. This is both foolish and futile. It will almost never happen. So many have tried this way and failed. It's far better to just go to the hospital and get the surgery done instead of attempting it on your own at home in your kitchen.

Besides, God *commanded* you to submit to the discipline of the church. He designed the church for your salvation; he knows what he's doing.

Don't walk into a trap. Fighting not only consists of hand-to-hand combat, it also involves *thinking*.

If there's one main characteristic of all battlefields, it's this: confusion and darkness rule the day. The tremendous noise, the unexpected movements of the enemy, not knowing how the battle is going, bursting shells all around you, losing communication with others on your own side, contradictory orders, the front line continually changing positions, uncooperative weather – all this and more make warfare one of the most difficult of human endeavors.

The enemy is relying on you to lose heart in the middle of all this confusion.

Army commanders are trained in how to use battlefield confusion itself as another weapon against their enemies. They try to create as much confusion as possible to mystify and demoralize the enemy, then strike hard at them when they are most helpless. On the other hand, they are trained to keep their cool in a battle; they can separate the confusion from the battle itself and keep on track with the objective.

Interestingly enough, the Bible describes our Christian warfare in the same way. One of the most important things we have to do is *stay alert* – because, since this world is a battlefield, there is going to be a tremendous amount of confusion and darkness. Most people won't have a clue about what's really going on around them; they will be easy targets for the enemy. God's people, however, *can* know what's going on if they keep their wits about them.

No one knows about that day or hour, not even the angels in Heaven, nor the Son, but only the Father. ***Be on guard! Be alert!*** You do not know when that time will come. (Mark 13:32-33)

And pray in the Spirit on all occasions with all kinds of prayers and requests. With this in mind, ***be alert*** and always keep on praying for all the saints. (Ephesians 6:18)

So then, let us not be like others, who are asleep, but ***let us be alert and self-controlled***. For those who sleep, sleep at night, and those who get drunk, get drunk at night. But since we belong to the day, let us be self-controlled, putting on faith and love as a breastplate, and the hope of salvation as a helmet. (1 Thessalonians 5:6-8)

Be self-controlled and alert. Your enemy the devil prowls around like a roaring lion looking for someone to devour. Resist him, standing firm in the faith, because you know that your brothers throughout the world are undergoing the same kind of sufferings. (1 Peter 5:8-9)

A Christian has to be on guard for various things:

<u>The presence of the enemy</u>. The enemy will almost always "masquerade as an angel of light." (2 Corinthians 11:14) He conceals his actions; he refuses to advertise his presence or his methods. It's up to you to know your enemy. You can be hit in any situation, through anybody – including friends and family. Even Peter, the Apostle in training, unwittingly served the devil's ends when he tried to keep Jesus from going to Jerusalem to be crucified. Jesus had to rebuke him sharply. "Get behind me, Satan! You are a stumbling block to me; you do not have in mind the things of God, but the things of men." (Matthew 16:23) At all times we have to be aware of what the enemy may be leading us into, and resist him at all costs, "in order that Satan might not outwit us. For we are not unaware of his schemes." (2 Corinthians 2:11)

Your own weak points. Just because you are converted doesn't mean that you're perfect yet. The process of making you ready to live with God in Heaven is just started. New converts are like young men in the military: they think that they can defeat anybody with one hand tied behind their backs! Well, the first fierce battle will humble any such pride. You will find yourself up against a ruthless foe who is out to destroy you in any way, usually by hitting your weakest points that you weren't even aware of. "Pride goes before destruction, a haughty spirit before a fall." (Proverbs 16:18) Your strength and wisdom is in God, not in yourself; it will take time to learn this on a practical level. What you have to get good at is tapping into God's power and wisdom at the right points, at the right time, to meet the problem situation as it arises. In other words, identify those weak points (time to get rid of your pride and take an honest look at yourself!) and fortify them with the Spirit's resources.

On track with the Mission. The battlefield is such a confusing and overpowering environment that the ordinary soldier often forgets what he's supposed to be doing, what with all the bombs and noise and casualties around him. So keep the Mission in mind at all times. Memorize it; train in it every day; do something toward it daily and check your progress. Jesus warned us that we will too often forget the Mission when life gets too good or too bad. "The one who received the seed that fell on rocky places is the man who hears the Word and at once receives it with joy. But since he has no root, he lasts only a short time. When trouble or persecution comes because of the Word, he quickly falls away. The one who received the seed that fell among the thorns is the man who hears the Word, but the worries of this life and the deceitfulness of wealth choke it, making it unfruitful." (Matthew 13:20-22) If you lose sense of your Mission, you won't end up in Heaven. *That's* the goal that you're supposed to be aiming for, whatever else may happen along the way.

The opportunity to strike. A good soldier is patient. He knows that there are times when it's not a good idea to stick his head up during a battle! He bides his time. That moment will come when the firing stops for a little bit, and now is the time to strike back. "Strike while the iron is hot," as the saying goes. So we "speak a word in season" – a word of comfort, rebuke or encouragement to the brother or sister in need. We give a "cup of cold water" to those who are thirsty, when God puts them into our lives to minister to. We confess our sins when God rebukes us, as David did, and find forgiveness right away. We are awake and aware when the conditions are ripe for our obedience, for prayer, for testimony, for patience and perseverance: "Be very careful, then, how you live – not as unwise but as wise, making the most of every opportunity, because the days are evil. Therefore do not be foolish, but understand what the Lord's will is." (Ephesians 5:15-17) Only someone who is well-trained and who understands the Mission will be aware of opportunities and jump on them before they disappear.

Being aware of the situation makes all the difference in the world between defeat and survival. But being able to interpret what's going on around us in the middle of a battle is a difficult thing. It was easy enough to learn the lessons from the blackboard in school; but out here in the world, one can't easily see those principles when so many things are going on. Most people can't remember how the lesson went; they weren't paying attention that day! Many more can't separate the "noise" of circumstances from the real issues.

David, for example, almost lost his faith, because he saw the wicked thriving and the righteous failing. The wicked were in power, and everywhere he went he was treated as a criminal and fugitive. He didn't understand how the God of justice would allow such a state of affairs. This confusion and darkness doesn't help us in our walk of faith! A little light on the situation, however, cleared everything up.

> When I tried to understand all this, it was oppressive to me till I entered the sanctuary of God; then I understood their final destiny. Surely you place them on slippery ground; you cast them down to ruin. How suddenly are they destroyed, completely swept away by terrors! As a dream when one awakes, so when you arise, O Lord, you will despise them as fantasies.
> When my heart was grieved and my spirit embittered, I was senseless and ignorant; I was a brute beast before you. Yet I am always with you; you hold me by my right hand. You guide me with your counsel, and afterward you will take me into glory. (Psalm 73:16-24)

Suddenly he saw the reality of God and that cleared the picture right up. It may not *look* like the wicked will fail in this world, but the light from Heaven will show it, for those who can see. Be aware.

Never fear the enemy. Most of warfare is mental. Armies are routinely beaten before anybody fires a shot. So are

Christians defeated when they sit down in the dust in despair, convinced that they can't go on and there isn't any hope left.

Napoleon made it a point never to tell his own troops how many of the enemy they were up against. To him, it didn't matter. He knew his men, and what they were capable of; if he felt that they were able to defeat even a larger foe, then he didn't hesitate to go to battle. He also knew how destructive a bad morale is to the fighting men; a positive attitude will double your fighting power. As a result, he won many battles even when heavily outnumbered.

We are fighting under a Commander who not only can't lose, but has already won the battle! Look where he is – above all powers and temptations, above sin and death, at God's right hand putting his enemies under his feet. Nobody can touch him; he rules *them* "with an iron scepter." (Psalm 2:9)

That's why he has no patience with "Christians" who run in fear and panic from the enemy. There is no reason for us to fear them and give up the battle.

> Because of the increase of wickedness, the love of most will grow cold, but *he who stands firm to the end will be saved.* (Matthew 24:12-13)

> No one who puts his hand to the plow and looks back is fit for service in the kingdom of God. (Luke 9:62)

That was the very sin of the early Israelites. When they were on the move to the Promised Land, they came to the borders of Canaan and sent in spies to find out what they were getting into. The spies reported back with good news and bad: the land *is* rich and abundant, they said, but there are giants in the land! Ten of those spies counseled caution; maybe now is not the time, they said, to go in.

God was furious! He had spent all those months in the desert training them in spiritual warfare, training them in his ways, and then they threw all that training away when they faced the enemy. In anger he denied them the privilege of the Promised Land; they didn't deserve it. He sent them back out into the desert to die.

> Nevertheless, as surely as I live and as surely as the glory of the LORD fills the whole earth, not one of the men who saw my glory and the miraculous signs I performed in Egypt and in the desert but who disobeyed me and tested me ten times – not one of them will ever see the land I promised on oath to their forefathers. No one who has treated me with contempt will ever see it. (Numbers 14:21-23)

God was angry with them because they forgot that their power was in God himself. *Never* look at how big the enemy is! God has promised us that, when we're on the march with him, he will go before us, destroy the opposition, and make the way plain.

> By day the LORD went ahead of them in a pillar of cloud to guide them on their way and by night in a pillar of fire to give them light, so that they could travel by day or night. Neither the pillar of cloud by day nor the pillar of fire by night left its place in front of the people. (Exodus 13:21-22)

Moses showed them at the Red Sea what will happen even when God seemingly leads us into a dead-end. While they were standing around in distress, wondering what in the world God had in mind by getting them into such a predicament, Moses alone knew what was coming.

> Do not be afraid. Stand firm and you will see the deliverance the LORD will bring you today. The Egyptians you see today you will never see again. The LORD will fight for you; you need only to be still. (Exodus 14:13-14)

People have a way of freezing up when they see trouble. There's nothing unnatural about fear, but one of the purposes of military training is to teach you how to deal with that fear. You shouldn't panic and run! Cowardice and surrender are not options for the people of God; there is absolutely no reason to turn tail and run when God himself is leading us against the enemy. Things may not *look* very promising, but you have all the firepower on your side; events will prove that. Paul endured suffering without wavering in his complete trust in God who could handle any problem.

> That is why I am suffering as I am. Yet I am not ashamed, because I know whom I have believed, and am convinced that he is able to guard what I have entrusted to him for that day. (2 Timothy 1:12)

Facing danger and doing your duty *will* take a lot of courage – but that's what war is all about. Courage often wins the battle. For example, when Moses died, Joshua got his new assignment: to be courageous and face his new task of leadership and war; both God and man encouraged him to this.

> No one will be able to stand up against you all the days of your life. As I was with Moses, so I will be with you; I will never leave you nor forsake you. Be strong and courageous, because you will lead these people to inherit the land I swore to their forefathers to give them. Be strong and very courageous. Be careful to obey all the law my servant Moses gave you; do not turn from it to the right or to the left, that you may be successful wherever you go. (Joshua 1:5-7)

Ecclesiastes has an interesting point to make about facing potential problems with courage.

> Whoever watches the wind will not plant; whoever looks at the clouds will not reap. As you do

not know the path of the wind, or how the body is formed in a mother's womb, so you cannot understand the work of God, the Maker of all things. Sow your seed in the morning, and at evening let not your hands be idle, for you do not know which will succeed, whether this or that, or whether both will do equally well. (Ecclesiastes 11:4-6)

Many people are naturally fearful and extremely reluctant to put themselves in a problem situation. Still, when God calls us to walk in a certain way, even if it involves suffering, our duty is to obey him – not find excuses about *what might happen*. If he told us to go a certain way, he will make that way open up before us even if there's a mountain in our way when we start. Just do what God commanded and you can't go wrong. Do you think God would send you out to defeat? Nothing stands in the way of God's purposes; only our lack of faith will bring everything to a halt.

Always keep the Mission in view. There are two areas in which troops are trained: general-purpose survival and fighting skills, and the Mission. A person may be a great fighter, but if he loses sight of what he is assigned to do, he will hurt things, not help things. We are here to do our Commander's will, not ours; in *that* is our victory.

The church's Mission is twofold: *first*, to help people crucify the sin that is still in them (this is called "sanctification"); and *second*, to help people get ready to live with a spiritual God in Heaven. All the training and resources that the Lord has given the church are designed with these two ends in view.

In today's church, however, people are doing just about everything except the Mission. They are having bazaars, social get-togethers, music festivals, celebrations, sports (one church that I know of offers cheerleading training!), entertainment, community projects – you name it, and someone is doing it. They claim to be doing all this in

Christ's name, but that's easy to say and hard to prove. Spirit-led training is to prepare us for *hard* times, not the easy times. We are supposed to be training for battle, not parties.

First, it is time to face our sin. This is the last thing that many people want to think about, even in church, but you have yet to truly see the holy God if you think that you don't need to work on this area in your life. Sin is the whole problem of mankind; now is not the time for denial! Those saints in the Bible who were already walking a life of righteousness were shocked at the utter holiness of God; the view put fear in their hearts over their own spiritual standing. They realized that they had a lot more to work on.

> In the year that King Uzziah died, I saw the Lord seated on a throne, high and exalted, and the train of his robe filled the temple ... And they were calling to one another: "Holy, holy, holy is the LORD Almighty; the whole earth is full of his glory." ... "Woe to me!" I cried. "I am ruined! For I am a man of unclean lips, and I live among a people of unclean lips, and my eyes have seen the King, the LORD Almighty." (Isaiah 6:1, 3, 5)

Isaiah, Moses, Daniel, Ezra, David, the Apostle John – these and many other righteous men and women humbled themselves before God and pleaded with him to make them *more* holy and righteous. They never thought themselves good enough to look God straight in the eyes. Sin stains the heart of flesh with a deep and fearful power; our constant life struggle will be against our own sinful nature.

> Consider him who endured such opposition from sinful men, so that you will not grow weary and lose heart. In your *struggle against sin*, you have not yet resisted to the point of shedding your blood. (Hebrews 12:3-4)

For the sinful nature desires what is contrary to the Spirit, and the Spirit what is contrary to the sinful nature. They are *in conflict* with each other, so that you do not do what you want. (Galatians 5:17)

As we fight to overcome this dreaded enemy, we appreciate more and more the effective weapons and training that God has given us to succeed. We understand better why Jesus was so focused on saving us from sin when he came. But we have to keep on track; we have to make this one of our two aims in life. We have to get serious about this issue of sin in us, because our acceptance into Heaven depends on it. Forget about this enemy, and you will fall in battle.

Come near to God and he will come near to you. Wash your hands, you sinners, and purify your hearts, you double-minded. Grieve, mourn and wail. Change your laughter to mourning and your joy to gloom. Humble yourselves before the Lord, and he will lift you up. (James 4:8-10)

The bottom line is that nobody is allowed into Heaven with sin in their hearts. Make it part of your daily agenda: "Forgive us our trespasses."

The *second* objective is just as vital – to get ready to live with God. As we are, we would never survive in Heaven; it's a spiritual place and we are *very* physically oriented. We know almost nothing about what it's like there; we know very little about God's ways.

When Jesus talked about the treasures of Heaven, for example, do you know what he was referring to?

Do not store up for yourselves treasures on earth, where moth and rust destroy, and where thieves break in and steal. But store up for yourselves treasures in Heaven, where moth and rust do not destroy, and where thieves do not break in and steal. For where your treasure is, there your heart will be also. (Matthew 6:19-21)

How many people have bothered to study what those treasures might be? Or have they read this passage over and over without any understanding at all of what he was talking about? I hope you realize that you have to *do* what he says here before you can benefit from those treasures!

God's world is spiritual, and you are physical. You have to change before you can live with God in Heaven.

> I declare to you, brothers, that flesh and blood cannot inherit the kingdom of God, nor does the perishable inherit the imperishable. (1 Corinthians 15:50)

This refers to our resurrection from the dead at the end of the world. But can we change now, ahead of time, in ways that will make us ready and willing to live with this spiritual God?

> Do not conform any longer to the pattern of this world, but be transformed by the renewing of your mind. Then you will be able to test and approve what God's will is – his good, pleasing and perfect will. (Romans 12:2)

> Since, then, you have been raised with Christ, set your hearts on things above, where Christ is seated at the right hand of God. Set your minds on things above, not on earthly things. For you died, and your life is now hidden with Christ in God. (Colossians 3:1-3)

Those who get rid of their sin will not be hurt when God destroys the wicked through disasters. Those who train themselves to think and hope for Heaven will not be hurt when the world collapses and takes down with it those who depend on it completely. You see, training in the Mission will save you through any danger.

Take the high ground. Another important military maxim is this: make sure that *you* choose the ground to fight on, not the enemy. If you decide where you want to fight, you can pick an area and the right conditions to help you win the battle. If the enemy chooses all that, you will probably lose, because everything will be in *his* favor.

Don't put yourself in a position to be beaten. At the simplest level, you need to make sure you are walking in righteousness and holiness so that you won't bring shame to the cause of Christ.

> May those who hope in you not be disgraced because of me, O Lord, the LORD Almighty; may those who seek you not be put to shame because of me, O God of Israel. (Psalm 69:6)

> Abstain from all appearance of evil.
> (1 Thessalonians 5:22, *KJV*)

The KJV reflects the original Greek the best here: though you may not be doing something wrong, you don't want to do anything that would even *look* like it may be wrong to those watching you. We don't want to give the unbelievers fuel for gossip and slander.

> In the same way, let your light shine before men, that they may see your good deeds and praise your Father in Heaven. (Matthew 5:16)

> Dear friends, I urge you, as aliens and strangers in the world, to abstain from sinful desires, which war against your soul. Live such good lives among the pagans that, though they accuse you of doing wrong,

they may see your good deeds and glorify God on the day he visits us. (1 Peter 2:11-12)

The Christian's life is a light on a hill, open for everybody to see. Not only do we want to "abstain from evil," we want to live in such a way that we are a positive, spiritual benefit to those around us. Though the pagan world will still hate us, they have no good reason for doing so. Christians are the perfect example of a useful, beneficial influence in any society. Would to God that every citizen in the community lived like that! The wicked may persecute us, but they'll be cutting the lifeblood out of their society as a result. They can't win wars like that! They're going to lose in the long run when they persecute us.

You are the light of the world. A city on a hill cannot be hidden. Neither do people light a lamp and put it under a bowl. Instead they put it on its stand, and it gives light to everyone in the house. (Matthew 5:14-15)

For you were once darkness, but now you are light in the Lord. Live as children of light (for the fruit of the light consists in all goodness, righteousness and truth) and find out what pleases the Lord. (Ephesians 5:8-10)

Another way to stick to the high ground is to refuse the enemy's invitation to fight on his turf. He of course is going to pick a place and time that will enable him to destroy you; avoid that at all costs. Are you savvy enough, however, to see those dangerous places? Job, for example, decided that he was much safer ignoring seductive females: "I made a covenant with my eyes not to look lustfully at a girl." (Job 31:1) And Proverbs teaches the same thing.

With persuasive words she led him astray; she seduced him with her smooth talk. All at once he followed her like an ox going to the slaughter, like a

> deer stepping into a noose till an arrow pierces his liver, like a bird darting into a snare, little knowing it will cost him his life.
>
> Now then, my sons, listen to me; pay attention to what I say. Do not let your heart turn to her ways or stray into her paths. Many are the victims she has brought down; her slain are a mighty throng. Her house is a highway to the grave, leading down to the chambers of death. (Proverbs 7:21-27)

If you buy the argument that "it's OK to look," you've just lost. *Nobody* wins that battle, because it's the best ground for the enemy to destroy you. "I tell you that anyone who looks at a woman lustfully has already committed adultery with her in his heart." (Matthew 5:28) In our society, too many women are looking and acting like prostitutes. Stay away from the immoral woman.

> I find more bitter than death the woman who is a snare, whose heart is a trap and whose hands are chains. The man who pleases God will escape her, but the sinner she will ensnare. (Ecclesiastes 7:26)

A more subtle way to "pick your battlefield" is to refuse to let the unbelievers force their anti-God philosophy on our society. The moral battles raging in our culture right now can be solved so easily if we would stop accepting the assumptions and standards that the unbelievers are using and stand on our own foundations. For example, homosexuality is a sin, an evil that should be rooted out of our society; the Bible says so. The current argument in our society, however, is revolving around the genetic inheritance of the homosexuals (which supposedly absolves them of responsibility and guilt!), and the undependability of the Bible in our modern culture to dictate hard and fast moral standards. Let's move the discussion to the facts, shall we? Let's talk about things that unbelievers don't want to face. **First**, we are *all* genetically disposed to sin! We inherited the sin nature from Adam and Eve. Homosexuals are no more free from responsibility than a murderer or thief who "can't help himself!" Their sin is just as destructive to society and family as murder is. **Second**, never accept an unbeliever's interpretation of the Bible. They are out to destroy its message, not honor and believe it. Keep preaching its plain and simple truth and don't get caught up in trying to defend "changing moral standards" or "contradictions in Scripture." The only contradictions are in the unbelievers' heads. Anybody with "eyes to see" will know that there's nothing wrong with the Bible; the problem is that sinners just don't want to believe it.

Another hot area of discussion is abortion. While the pro-abortionists push the church on "protecting the mother's health," and "rape victims," and the "rights of the woman" – why aren't we targeting the *real* reason for all these abortions? People want unlimited sex, free from moral restraints, with anybody they want at any time. They want to throw away the Bible's standards of marriage and purity and live in continuous lust. And that, as we learned in Biology 101, results in unwanted children. So this discussion is *not* about the fringe problem pregnancies, nor should we Christians limit our focus to the murders of the babies. It's about today's immoral lifestyle. Fight that, and you're hitting the root problem. Ah, but you say, we can't do that because the government won't let us talk about the Bible's morals. Well, that proves my point: that's the result of the enemy setting up the battlefield to help *him* win. It's time for us to reintroduce the Bible to the discussion. That's the one weapon that the enemy can't tolerate.

Creation is a third area in which modern Christians are thoroughly confused, mainly because they are accepting too many of the assumptions of the unbelieving world. Science reigns supreme in our culture; even Christians have bowed their knee to the dictates of science as it proclaims the truth about how this world came into existence. In fact, Christians also reinterpret Genesis to make it fit with scientific "laws" to make it more palatable to the modern man. The problem here is obvious: science can't back up its arrogant claims about the beginning of the world because *they weren't there to verify their claims.*   Has nobody asked the obvious question here? I thought science was based on observation! The only thing that science has to go on here are theories, and theories don't make it fact.   The problem is that these theories directly contradict the Bible's testimony of what happened at the beginning. We, in fact, have an eyewitness of Creation – the Spirit of God (Genesis 1:2) who testified of what he saw in the report he gave Moses (see 2 Peter 1:20-21 on how a prophet gets his information!). We Christians have a much stronger position than any scientist could have. And why is Creation such an important subject? Because it solves the problem of who made the world, and who it belongs to, and our relationship to him, and the necessity of Judgment Day! (*See* **The Bible Explains Creation** *for a fuller discussion on this subject.*)

All this is to show that Christians aren't very savvy on the battlefield. If we are losing the battle in these and other areas, it's because (in fear of not being "accepted" or "respectable") we've accepted the assumptions of the wicked and are fighting on the battlefield of *their* choosing – and losing as a result.

> For the people of this world are more shrewd in dealing with their own kind than are the people of the light. (Luke 16:8)

One more aspect of "taking the high ground." Remember that you are only one soldier in God's army. Though you have been called to do your duty, and your actions in life will make a difference, your hope is not in yourself. God is your power and wisdom. There are times when you have to do what he assigned for you, but there are other times when you need to step back and "wait on the Lord" to do his part, because that's the only solution to the problem. This takes a lot of discernment, patience, and faith. We are so eager to jump in and solve things ourselves that we forget that we aren't able to solve life's most serious problems.

For example, Paul talks about relying on spiritual weapons that will decisively defeat the enemy.

> For though we live in the world, we do not wage war as the world does. The weapons we fight with are not the weapons of the world. On the contrary, they have divine power to demolish strongholds. (2 Corinthians 10:3-4)

James backs this up by showing how futile it is to use our weapons, when God's weapons are designed for the job.

> My dear brothers, take note of this: Everyone should be quick to listen, slow to speak and slow to become angry, *for man's anger does not bring about the righteous life that God desires*. (James 1:19-20)

In confirmation of everything we've been talking about so far, Peter counsels us to be alert in light of the approaching storm and rely on those skills that will make us strong and ready for battle: not the world's solutions, but God's solutions.

> The end of all things is near. Therefore be clear-minded and self-controlled so that you can pray. Above all, *love* each other deeply, because *love covers over a multitude of sins*. (1 Peter 4:7-8)

Instead of trying desperately to manage things on our own, we do what God tells us to do and *trust him* to take care of the impossible. We can't even save ourselves, let alone change the world. We do have a Rock to stand on, however: the peace and righteousness and power and wisdom of Christ, as he carries us through the storm. Rely on that, and you will never lose.

Do not be anxious about anything, but in everything, by prayer and petition, with thanksgiving, present your requests to God. And the peace of God, which transcends all understanding, will guard your hearts and your minds in Christ Jesus. (Philippians 4:6-7)

Maintain a strong defense. There are times when we have to go on the defensive; the enemy is attacking us, and we have to have a strong fortress to hide in and defend ourselves. We simply don't have the strength to fight them out in the open field without some help.

The saying in military circles is that a good fortress is equivalent to six times your troop strength. In other words, 1000 troops defending a fort can hold out against 6000 attacking soldiers. There's a lot of strength in those stones! In fact, in most battles of history where fortresses fell, the defenders surrendered because they *thought* they were going to be overrun. It was a problem with morale; they didn't understand the strength of their position. They gave up too soon.

God has wisely provided a strong place for his people in times of war: *himself.* In this case, the strength-factor skyrockets. *Nobody can reach you when you are resting in God.* He is your Rock, your fortress, your shield against the enemy. There is no enemy, no weapon, no strategy good enough to bring you down when you take refuge in Christ, no matter how persistent the enemy might be.

Do not be afraid, Abram. I am your shield, your very great reward. (Genesis 15:1)

The LORD is my rock, my fortress and my deliverer; my God is my rock, in whom I take refuge. He is my shield and the horn of my salvation, my stronghold. I call to the LORD, who is worthy of praise, and I am saved from my enemies. (Psalm 18:2-3)

Unfortunately, Christians are guilty of giving up too soon in the battle. They don't understand the strength of their position in Christ.

So do not worry, saying, 'What shall we eat?' or 'What shall we drink?' or 'What shall we wear?' For the pagans run after all these things, and your Heavenly Father knows that you need them. But seek first his kingdom and his righteousness, and all these things will be given to you as well. Therefore do not worry about tomorrow, for tomorrow will worry about itself. Each day has enough trouble of its own. (Matthew 6:31-34)

Do not be afraid of those who kill the body but cannot kill the soul. Rather, be afraid of the One who can destroy both soul and body in hell. Are not two sparrows sold for a penny? Yet not one of them will fall to the ground apart from the will of your Father. And even the very hairs of your head are all numbered. So don't be afraid; you are worth more than many sparrows. (Matthew 10:28-31)

For I am convinced that neither death nor life, neither angels nor demons, neither the present nor the future, nor any powers, neither height nor depth, nor anything else in all creation, will be able to separate us from the love of God that is in Christ Jesus our Lord. (Romans 8:38)

In fact, the very trials that cause so much despair and fear in us are designed by our Father in Heaven to *strengthen* our faith and spiritual maturity. In his hands, they are blessings, not curses. That's how much our God is in control of things.

Oddly enough, one of the greatest fears of the Christian is that, if we do *exactly* what God tells us to do, things won't work. It doesn't look reasonable; we know how the world works, and this looks as if it's flying in the face of all possibility. God is asking us to walk on water! Little do we realize that the Creator knows how to overrule the principles of this world. If he's telling us to walk on water, it's because he has a more certain path for us to walk in than the troublesome roads of this world. The Cross, believe it or not, is the pathway to life. Stay in *his* paths and you can't be beaten.

Our spiritual position in Christ is specially designed to protect us from spiritual dangers (not necessarily physical dangers!). While everyone else believes the lies of the Enemy, and unbelievers give themselves over to materialism, and they trust in their own wisdom (and they're dying as a result), Christians are building their lives on God's Word, on the treasures of Heaven, and on the wisdom and leading of the Spirit. Then when the physical disasters happen, the unbelievers collapse and the Christians are still standing. Our defense proves stronger than theirs in the end.

Paul describes our defensive armor in Ephesians 6. Like a fortress, we surround ourselves with protective spiritual realities and trust in them to keep the enemy at bay.

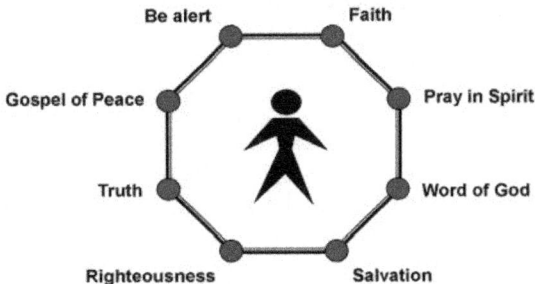

If we don't keep each point strong and in good working order, however, we create a weak point in our defensive shield. The enemy is always looking for our weak points.

Once he spots it (and he can probably find it sooner than you will be aware of it yourself) he will hit you *there* with his full force.

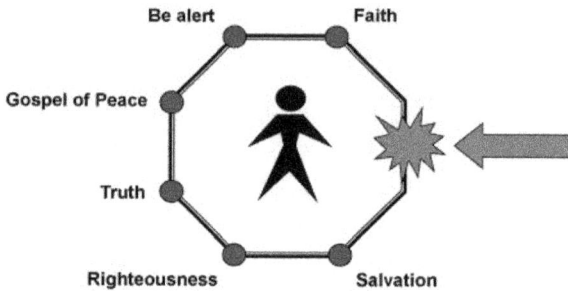

That's why it is vitally important to be constantly alert and on the defensive. You have to train daily, in all vital areas, if you hope to survive. You never know when or where the next attack might come.

Hold your position. Remember that you are in Christ's army, and he is the Commander. This is the *militant church*, not an entertainment center. To survive, you must train yourself to listen carefully to his orders and follow them to the letter. He has a Mission, and your duty is to do your part to help him build *his* Kingdom. You are not supposed to be serving your own purposes in life.

So many people miss this fact. Even in church, they aren't happy unless everything is designed to suit them and their tastes. They are totally self-centered. They condemn the leaders when they don't set things up in a way that will please and entertain them. They judge other people by the standard of whether those people are nice to them. If the church makes them feel good, they'll stay; if things in the church make them feel uncomfortable or pressed, they'll either complain or leave. One recent news item quoted a church-goer and her expectations of church: "Just going to church and everything ... it's very calming, and everyone is nice."

I can imagine how long an army recruit would last in basic training with an attitude like that.

If this is all that church is to you, you are in for a rude awakening when the enemy hits you ruthlessly with disaster. Suddenly events all around you are exploding like bomb-shells; there is nobody near who can help you because they're in the middle of their own troubles; you are confused about what is going on; and in despair you "cry out to the Lord in your distress." However, since you weren't careful to train yourself in maintaining communications with your supply line, you won't hear back from him. Confusion and despair deepen. You try this and that to solve the problem and nothing works, since you aren't trained for dealing with hardship. Finally, since God obviously isn't listening to you, you retreat from your position in defeat and go back to the world's way.

You just failed on two counts: *first*, you failed to learn your lessons on living by faith ahead of time, before disaster hits. *Second*, you failed the Lord and the church by leaving your place in the front line. Now the people around you are dangerously exposed to enemy attack, because you left your place and there's a gap in the line. Depending on what happens to the church because of your cowardice, the Lord will have to change plans and reform the line in order to save others. *All this because you failed him in the hour of battle.*

God has little patience for cowards, traitors and deserters. Read again what he has to say about cowards in Revelation 21:8. He told us this would be a war, he held training programs to get us ready, and he does *not* like people ignoring him.

There's just too much at stake here: God's glory, the safety and well-being of the church, the defeat of the enemy, meeting the Mission objectives. Why should he reward you when others who were faithful and did their duty suffered in the line of duty? *They* are the ones who will be rewarded!

> These are they who have come out of the great tribulation; they have washed their robes and made them white in the blood of the Lamb. Therefore, they are before the throne of God and serve him day and night in his temple; and he who sits on the throne will spread his tent over them. (Revelation 7:14-15)

I think that Isaac Watts' hymn says it wonderfully.

> Must I be carried to the skies
> On flowery beds of ease,
> While others fought to win the prize,
> And sailed through bloody seas?

Read the rest of that hymn and you will get the sense of a Christian soldier ready and willing to do his or her duty.

In times of hardship and trial, we get hurt – and naturally we are inclined to look around for a way of getting out of that trial. But at no time are we permitted to leave our post or disobey the clear commands of our Lord. Saul learned this the hard way. When God gave him a clear command to totally destroy the enemy, he disobeyed; it seemed wasteful to him to destroy *everything* when the Israelites were in such need. Well, he found out that we are not at liberty to change our orders for any reason.

> Does the LORD delight in burnt offerings and sacrifices as much as in obeying the voice of the LORD? To obey is better than sacrifice, and to heed is better than the fat of rams. For rebellion is like the sin of divination, and arrogance like the evil of idolatry. Because you have rejected the Word of the LORD, he has rejected you as king. (1 Samuel 15:22-23)

When God decides that it's time for you to suffer for his sake, step up to do your duty and *suffer for his sake*. Any job in God's army is an honor! Each assignment is vital to the life of the church; every responsibility that God gives you, no matter how difficult or unpleasant, helps meet the Lord's objectives as he builds his Kingdom.

Blessed are you when people insult you, persecute you and falsely say all kinds of evil against you because of me. Rejoice and be glad, because great is your reward in Heaven, for in the same way they persecuted the prophets who were before you. (Matthew 5:11-12)

Also, when he gives you a job to do, don't you dare move from your position until he gives you clear orders to do so. The battle depends on you holding your position; others depend on your faithfulness to your duty. You can't excuse yourself just because times are hard, or you are bored, or there doesn't seem to be any success, or you're getting shot at all the time. You only *think* you can't make it. Actually God knows exactly how much you can take, and he will support you (many times without your direct knowledge) until he decides that you may withdraw.

No temptation has seized you except what is common to man. And God is faithful; he will not let you be tempted beyond what you can bear. But when you are tempted, he will also provide a way out so that you can stand up under it. (1 Corinthians 10:13)

Let us not become weary in doing good, for at the proper time we will reap a harvest if we do not give up. (Galatians 6:9)

Consider him who endured such opposition from sinful men, so that you will not grow weary and lose heart. (Hebrews 12:3)

Time to get ready

If this seems like a long discussion, it's because today's church is, for the most part, *not* in a state of readiness for war; it's anything but ready. Most Christians aren't thinking in terms of war at all. That's why they'll be such an easy kill for the enemy when war comes.

You may not like the idea of war, and I'd like to be able to tell you that you will never have to use these principles of war in your life. But I know too much about how the world works; and besides the Lord himself tells us that we will have troubles. You simply *have* to learn war if you want to survive. There is no other way.

Church Work

In our present culture, churches are designed to entertain and satisfy the customers. In case you think that's too harsh a criticism, consider the following:

- Entertainment is a big factor in church services: full bands, drop-down screens for sing-along (it reminds me of the karaoke restaurants), using secular music in worship, full TV and radio capabilities for broadcasting the service, and specially trained experts hired to make sure all this happens flawlessly in a professional manner.

- People "support" the ministry by paying for multi-million dollar church properties; mega-churches boast thousands of members, drive-in services, ATM's for tithing; churches advertise special counseling for single parents, divorcees, and stressed-out truck drivers to draw the crowds. There are churches for cowboys, for Harley riders, for macho men, for Las Vegas showgirls (I'm describing actual churches that I've either seen or read about!) Churches offer cheerleading training, bingo games, community picnics, steam-cleaning services – it's like reading the Yellow Pages in the telephone book! People feel that they had better get their money's worth or they're going to go to another church across town that *will* give them what they want!

- Pastors have to be entertainers and salesmen. They hold people's attention with jokes and stories, they plead for money, they make people feel good about themselves; they know how to manipulate crowds. The qualifications that churches demand from their pastors are ridiculous; one church's "job description" extended to a list of over fifty demands, and very few of them were from the Bible! And

145

on the other side of that coin, there's a high rate of "burn out" in the pastorate as people struggle to maintain the world's idea of a church. Of course, most pastors insist on being taken care of, too – six-figure salaries are often standard for many beginning pastors in churches these days. They wouldn't do it for any less.

- If things get too close for comfort – when the pastor or elder starts confronting an individual about their particular sins and shortcomings – that individual usually gets offended and leaves the church. They have no intention of being treated as if they are sinners. Church is for getting people to feel good, to have a good time, to be over-comers, to be commended, to be "affirmed" in what they are doing. People aren't there to change.

Leave it to Americans to turn church into another Hollywood, complete with glitter and wealth and hidden immorality! The long and the short of it is this: the church is competing with the world. They try everything they can to draw in more people, build up the income, expand their physical assets, hold people's attention, and keep them from leaving. Everything in the church is consumer-driven; keep the customers happy and they'll keep coming back and giving more money. We have to pay for these big buildings and enormous expenses, so we have to keep the people coming and donating. There is hardly any difference at all between the modern church and a business: the expenses drive the program. In the meantime, little or nothing is being done about the Problem. It would be better to tear it all down and start over.

What usually happens in today's churches is *not* the Mission of the church. We have come a long way from God's original model. In fact, if you would put the modern American church up against the church described in the book of Acts, you wouldn't know we were talking about the same thing!

People will do what they want, and they won't be talked out of something when they're having so much fun with it. So I have little hope of getting through to all these people in the modern church – that is, until a catastrophe happens. Then when millions are dying from the plague, and society collapses from financial ruin, and war is ripping apart our civilization, people will not be in the mood for jokes and fun and games. They will want answers. They won't go to the entertainer for help; they will go to the **prophet**. *What can we do,* they will plead, *to appease this God of wrath?!*

I realize that I'm describing disaster on a national scale, which may or may not happen in your lifetime (it *is* happening right now in other countries, by the way). But churches are so out of touch with reality that they are, for the most part, incapable of handling even the smaller-scale disasters that happen to individuals and families. Their ministries focus on keeping the ship afloat in calm waters, in good times, in the midst of little or no troubles. When someone in genuine trouble comes along, many "Christians" turn their backs on them and hope they go away. I've seen it happen. Whereas in the early church the Christians sold homes and land to help each other out of difficulties, modern Christians would rather quit their church and go somewhere else than confront that kind of need. We aren't set up at all for disaster; we like to let the government take care of that!

There needs to be a fundamental shift in our outlook. The church's Mission is not to entertain people, nor to build empires. Our Mission is *to get people ready for Heaven.* In order to accomplish this Mission, we have to get "lean and mean." There is no need for any program in a church that doesn't directly support that Mission. It's time to give back to the world what it's good at (partying, playing, entertaining, and having fun), and focus on what only the church is good at: God and salvation. We need to overhaul the church, from top to bottom, throwing out what we don't need and putting into place what we do need. Right now our churches are known for doing *anything* to get people to come; what we need is a new image – we are a *spiritual hospital.* Come, if you're sick, to get healed.

If you live in a rural area, you may know the frustration of going to the local hospital and finding out that they can't help you; they aren't equipped for the kind of emergency you are bringing to them. They have to put you in an ambulance and drive you hundreds of miles to a bigger hospital where they can take care of that kind of thing.

There are millions of people in this country that have tried to find help in their local churches and left disappointed. The churches aren't set up to handle their cases. When people are having trouble with their spouses, the real problem is *sin*. When people are struggling financially, the real problem is *sin*. Arguments in church? – sin. When people have six-digit incomes, two homes, and three cars, and still can't find meaning in life, the real problem is *sin*. Yet church leaders aren't willing to face those people about their sinful, rebellious natures. It's true, many churches talk about sin in an abstract way, but almost nobody is willing to confront it directly. We live in a no-fault culture, and churches have basically bought into that philosophy when dealing with its members. Thus the problem is never solved.

But if you have a church that approaches its ministry in this way –

- This is God's world, and we are his servants.

- The Bible is the only truth that we go by.

- We are sinners; our greatest need is to be delivered of our sin.

- God deserves our all – strength, mind, body.

- The goal is to leave this world and live with God; and we have a lot to do to get ready for this.

- Union with Christ, through his Spirit, is the key to our goal.

… this church knows where it's going. It's not set up for fun and games; it is set up for getting people out of this world and into the next world. It has a clear, well-defined, achievable Mission that everyone can understand. *This* church can really help people; those in need of help can come here and get real help for their problems.

It takes a lot of work, study in the Bible, and foresight and perseverance to set up a church that fits in so well with the spiritual needs of its members. It certainly doesn't happen by accident! It also requires the leaders to have a healthy fear of the Lord of the Church, so that they will be careful to set things up in a way that will please him.

Unfaithful stewards who aren't leading the sheep home are in for a rough time on Judgment Day.

We are told that Jesus came to "save his people from their sin." (Matthew 1:21) Jesus himself told us that he is away right now, preparing a place to live with him in Heaven; someday he's going to come back and take us there. (John 14:2-3) It shouldn't be any surprise, therefore, to discover that the work of *his* Church will focus on those two great goals. We ought to be able to clearly see, when we enter *his* Church, how well-equipped it is for that purpose. *That's* the kind of church I want to be part of.

Organization

Christ's church is organized from the top down. In the church's government there is only one Head – Christ himself. Democracy has no place in the church. We aren't supposed to vote on morality, or salvation issues, or what to believe in the Word, or what the church needs to do in its work of the Kingdom; we are supposed to seek his will and do that *with no questions*. He is the Sovereign Monarch; he is, as Peter describes, a despot (δεσποτης – 2 Peter 2:1) – in the good sense. He is not interested in our opinions; we've messed up our lives enough following our own will and ideas. He is interested only in our obedience. Disobedience brings condemnation. (See Matthew 25 for examples of man's opinionated excuses and Christ's kingly wrath.)

Whatever government the Church will have, therefore, will be a system of passing down Christ's will to all the members – it is *not* intended to let them choose their own ways! No wonder, therefore, that the Apostles and Prophets (the *source* of the truth that we go by – the Scriptures, the printed will of Christ) and pastors and teachers (the *means* whereby the Scriptures are given to the Church) figure so largely in the structure of the Church's operations. Once you have this principle down, it's just a matter of learning God's will, doing it, and correcting those who fail to carry out God's will.

There are three levels of government in Christ's Kingdom.

- *First*, the **Apostles and Prophets** got their authority from God himself. Their duty was more than simply to wander around the world preaching and starting churches. God gave them the **Word**, they wrote it down, and they passed it on to us. We now possess the Word of God by their efforts. That's why the work of the Prophets and Apostles is so fundamental to the work of the Church. [2]

> Consequently, you are no longer foreigners and aliens, but fellow citizens with God's people and members of God's household, ***built on the foundation of the Apostles and Prophets,*** with Christ Jesus himself as the chief cornerstone. (Ephesians 2:19-20)

We honor that authority by learning and doing what they passed on to us from Christ. These are the very words of God. In other words (in case it hasn't hit you yet) *we do not deviate from the truth of the Bible.* We are not free to add to it or subtract from it. It is true just as it stands. The Bible doesn't need our present culture to improve it. It is truth for all ages, all people everywhere, just as it reads. People who would water down or do away with passages in the Bible are enemies of Christ – and the church needs to identify them as such.

> I warn everyone who hears the words of the prophecy of this book: If anyone adds anything to them, God will add to him the plagues described in this book. And if anyone takes words away from this book of prophecy, God will take away from him his share in the tree of life and in the holy city, which are described in this book. (Revelation 22:18-19)

This Word – both Old and New Testaments – is what God has given his church through all ages to be saved from sin and death. It is perfectly adequate to do that job. It is the full statement of our faith and practice; we need nothing else for the

---

[2] A fascinating example of Jesus "doing as his father David had done" is found in the Gospels that show us Christ choosing his disciples. He was literally collecting the "materials" for the spiritual Temple he is building; they are the "foundation" that he would build his church upon. See Matthew 4:18-22.

purpose. With the work of the Spirit, all of God's people can understand its message and be saved – they need nothing else but the Word of God.

- *Second*, **pastors and teachers** are also assigned to their jobs; Christ gave these functions to the Church for her growth and well-being. Where did we get the notion that these functions in the church are hired positions? To treat a pastor or teacher in Christ's church as an employee is to reject Christ's authority. Pastors usually get a paycheck, but that doesn't make the shepherd an employee of the sheep – such an idea is absurd. Pastors and teachers are Christ's workers, shepherds assigned to the job of caring for Christ's flock. The pay that a pastor receives is compensation for his hard work for the flock, and imposed on that flock by the Lord of the Church.

In the same way, the Lord has commanded that those who preach the gospel should receive their living from the gospel. (1 Corinthians 9:14)

The elders who direct the affairs of the church well are worthy of double honor, especially those whose work is preaching and teaching. For the Scripture says, "Do not muzzle the ox while it is treading out the grain," and "The worker deserves his wages." (1 Timothy 5:17-18)

Shepherds are ultimately answerable to the Chief Shepherd alone. They are to do the job he gave them to do, as he describes it in his Word. To hold them responsible to do what church members dream up as a replacement for God's job description in the Bible is to shackle them with trivia that prevents them from doing *Christ's* will.

So the Twelve gathered all the disciples together and said, "It would not be right for us to neglect the ministry of the Word of God in order to wait on tables. Brothers, choose seven men from among you who are known to be full of the Spirit and wisdom. We will turn this responsibility over to them and will give our attention to prayer and the ministry of the Word." (Acts 6:2-4)

Their allegiance and obedience is *upward* in the hierarchy, to Christ – their duties downward to the flock.

> Be shepherds of God's flock that is under your care, serving as overseers – not because you must, but because you are willing, as God wants you to be; not greedy for money, but eager to serve; not lording it over those entrusted to you, but being examples to the flock. And when the Chief Shepherd appears, you will receive the crown of glory that will never fade away. (1 Peter 5:1-4)

The authority of a leader is not an empty concept. He has the right and the duty to use the Word of God boldly in the church, applying it to people's hearts as necessary. If he shies away from his duty to confront sinners with their sin, he isn't doing them any favors and he is opening up the whole church to confusion about the seriousness of sin. And if he beats the sheep, the Chief Shepherd is going to have harsh words for him. So at times he has to be firm and confrontational, and at other times gentle and compassionate. His goal at all times, however, is to lead the flock to salvation in Christ. We *have* to take him seriously; he is Christ's representative.

> I will give you the keys of the kingdom of Heaven; whatever you bind on earth will be bound in Heaven, and whatever you loose on earth will be loosed in Heaven. (Matthew 16:19)

> This is why I write these things when I am absent, that when I come I may not have to be harsh in my use of authority – the authority the Lord gave me for building you up, not for tearing you down. (2 Corinthians 13:10)

The leaders of the church are responsible for *teaching* and *discipline*. They are to use the Word alone for teaching; as we've seen, God's people need only God's Word, and all of

God's Word, to be saved and prepared for Heaven. The leaders are responsible to become well-trained in the Bible so that they can give the flock what it needs.

Therefore every teacher of the Law who has been instructed about the kingdom of Heaven is like the owner of a house who brings out of his storeroom new treasures as well as old. (Matthew 13:52)

Do your best to present yourself to God as one approved, a workman who does not need to be ashamed and who correctly handles the Word of truth. (2 Timothy 2:15)

Discipline involves many things; correcting troublemakers in the church is only one of its aspects. Perhaps if you think of the military you will begin to appreciate its fuller meaning. In order to prepare soldiers for battle, the officers make the recruits drill and practice and drill and practice until they can do it in their sleep! This continual training is for a purpose: on the battlefield, a soldier has to do the *right* thing *immediately*, or he will die. There is no time to study in the middle of a battle. The right action has to be instinctive. In the same way, the leaders of the church must train the members in the truths and practice of Christianity. Then when the time comes and we are called upon to defend ourselves against the enemy, we will do the right thing without hesitation or doubt.

Leaders are not to be subject to the whims of the discontented members of the flock, because in every group there are those who will target the leaders to take the spotlight off themselves. They demand that the leader do their will, and in the process create no end of confusion and trouble.

Do not entertain an accusation against an elder unless it is brought by two or three witnesses. (1 Timothy 5:19)

When an elder sins it's a public matter; the church should proceed carefully to rebuke an elder. Most of the complaints against leaders, however, come from ignorance, rebellion, and the need for a scapegoat – and should be dismissed as such. It's easy to hurl accusations against the leaders when you're sitting in the back row, but they are almost never true. Moses had continual complaints and accusations thrown against him, all undeserved. Leaders carry burdens that the members know little about – not only the commands from the Lord about things that must be done in the ministry of the church, but the problems of all the members of the church weigh on them also. Criticisms from ignorant members only make things harder for them.

Obey your leaders and submit to their authority. They keep watch over you as men who must give an account. Obey them so that their work will be a joy, *not a burden*, for that would be of no advantage to you. (Hebrews 13:17)

• *Third*, Christ has given **spiritual gifts** to various members of the church. In many of today's churches, the subject of spiritual gifts is little understood and almost never explored. Preachers are always hammering on the subject – "everyone has a gift they should be using" – but members, though willing, have no idea how to proceed in even identifying their gift, let alone using it. And then you often have that insecure pastor who would really rather you *didn't* use your gift because it would take away from his own power and influence in the church!

The gifts are designed to distribute Christ's grace to the flock. They are channels through which the King influences and blesses his subjects from Heaven. The gifts that Christ gives to the church[3] are listed in Romans 12:6-8, 1 Corinthians 12:8-10, Ephesians 4:11, and 1 Peter 4:10-11. A spiritual gift brings others into the presence of Christ. It makes the spiritual world of God more real to people so that they are confronted, encouraged, and enabled with the presence of God in their lives. It aids in worship, the life of faith, seeing the truth of the Word, and

---

[3] This brings up an important point – you can't claim that every natural skill you might have is a "spiritual gift." Christ knows what his church needs, and he enables the bearer of the spiritual gift to do the work he is after. You may have a natural artistic ability; but "art" is not one of the spiritual gifts. His Word, remember, reveals the truth to us and directs the affairs of the church, not our opinions or feelings.

obedient living. As you can see, the jobs of "pastor" and "teacher" are not the only means that Christ spiritually enriches his flock. It's critical for the spiritual well-being of the flock that every member does his duty and helps build Christ's Kingdom.

Church members often go into a panic when you tell them they have to follow the leadership of the church. Their excuse (which may be just a cover-up for an insubordinate attitude) is that the leaders are fallible too. How are they going to make sure the leaders do the right thing? What if the leaders go wrong? In other words, they don't trust anybody else's judgment except their own, especially when it comes to someone telling them what to believe or how to live.

This is usually just a cover-up for their own unwillingness to follow anybody. We can tell because of their faulty logic: since it's *possible* that leaders may go wrong (they say), then let's not have a government with *anybody* in charge. Or, let's *all* of us be in charge. Or at least make it possible for us to get rid of someone we don't like.

The Bible, however, doesn't authorize us to throw the baby out with the bathwater. Yes, it's possible for sinful men to take a perfectly good system of church government and ruin things. That doesn't mean, however, that we do away with church government. The Bible does give us safeguards against sinful leaders. But the Lord commanded us to *submit to his form of government*, even if we have to discipline a few people along the way who abuse the system – including the leaders.

To be a leader in the church is a sensitive and perilous role. Though we do it in humility, remembering our own weaknesses, we also must do it with the authority that Christ gave us and not let others reject our role simply because we are sinful men. It's like the policeman who stops us for speeding. We had better do what he says – the Law stands behind him and gives him his authority – even though he probably speeds occasionally too during his off hours! The teacher of the Word has his own sins (which he should be working on!), but to reject the ministry of that teacher is to reject the Lord who sent him. Nevertheless, the leader is under a double burden of his own soul as well as the souls of others.

> Not many of you should presume to be teachers, my
> brothers, because you know that we who teach will be
> judged more strictly. (James 3:1)

A real limitation in the leadership of the church is that they can't
see into a person's heart as Christ can. They may think that a member
is being obstinate and rebellious against the teaching of the Word,
when actually that person may be struggling with the issue secretly and
going to Christ about it continually. That's why leaders need to stick to
their job and let Christ do his.

The options available to church leaders are limited *due to their
inability to change the sinner's heart.* Even when there's sin in the
church, the leaders can only bring it out into the open; and, if the sinner
won't repent, they must put him out of the church. Paul told the
Corinthian church to see a certain person to the door, and don't let him
back in until he repents. Such a "punishment" seems light until you
realize who will actually do the punishing. It's not the church's job to
punish; they are simply to address the situation and deal with it.

> When you are assembled in the name of our Lord Jesus
> and I am with you in spirit, and the power of our Lord Jesus
> is present, hand this man over to Satan, so that the sinful
> nature may be destroyed and his spirit saved on the day of
> the Lord. (1 Corinthians 4:4-5)

You can learn the lessons of Christ the easy way or the hard way.
Satan is a cruel taskmaster; a rebel will wish many times, before the
ordeal is over, that he had done it the easy way and submitted to the
leaders of the church! The church, in doing its duty, leaves any
appropriate punishment up to God, who alone knows how to bring the
sinner back to repentance.

Families have parents, governments have prime ministers and
presidents, classrooms have teachers, and yet many churches have –
nobody. We all understand the importance of leadership in all aspects
of life except, for some strange reason, in the church. There *we all* like
to rule. Every Tom, Dick and Harry is an expert in the Bible and
church doings, and they're not satisfied unless they have a major say in
what goes on there.

If Jesus doesn't rule in his church you will have certain disaster. Ruling ourselves is the very essence of sin; it's rebellion against Christ's rule. It's the reason the world is in such a mess as it is. It's the reason God has reacted with such anger and cursed the human race with death. If church members refuse to accept the King's government, as it is revealed in his Word, then they are cutting themselves off from the King and can only expect him to visit them in his wrath, with his Heavenly army behind him. The Bible makes this very plain.

> I have installed my King on Zion, my holy hill ... Therefore, you kings, be wise; be warned, you rulers of the earth. Serve the Lord with fear and rejoice with trembling. Kiss the Son, lest he be angry and you be destroyed in your way, for his wrath can flare up in a moment. Blessed are all who take refuge in him. (Psalm 6:10-12)

Many churches have no intention of submitting themselves to Christ's rule over them. They also think that they have a wonderful church going; they aren't in the least impressed with the Bible's threats and so they ignore them. They seem to be blissfully unaware that Christ has written "Ichabod" over the door of their assembly and he is no longer there among them. They are also blind to the fact, or they choose not to see, that the Mission isn't being accomplished among them. Since they refuse to submit to the Word, the Spirit isn't saving them from their sin and they aren't being prepared for life in Heaven. They are earth-bound and destined to be destroyed in the end. Lawlessness brings anarchy and spiritual disaster on a church.

Family

There's another problem that has to be addressed in a church if we want this program to work. Being the modern democratic individuals that we are, we like our freedom – from everyone. Our modern society, in fact, is specially designed to insulate and isolate you even from your next-door neighbor. In past centuries the community was stronger than it is now. People in the same neighborhood, even in the same town, knew each other and related to each other. Now in our modern world, we have isolated ourselves to our living rooms and have cut out even the extended family from our pastimes and pursuits.

This same attitude has come into the church. We are a far cry from the original Apostolic church, or even the church down through the centuries in other societies. Christians put up with each other only for an hour or two during Sunday and then return to their safe haven at home. There are many reasons for this, not least the pull of the world with its entertainments and pleasures that compete with the church for our time and attention. The result is that we know almost nothing about our brothers and sisters at church, nor do we care much about them.

Just to show you that this isn't normal, let's look at a passage from Acts that describes the life of the early church.

> They devoted themselves to the Apostles' teaching and to the fellowship, to the breaking of bread and to prayer. Everyone was filled with awe, and many wonders and miraculous signs were done by the Apostles. All the believers were together and had everything in common. Selling their possessions and goods, they gave to anyone as he had need. Every day they continued to meet together in the temple courts. They broke bread in their homes and ate together with glad and sincere hearts, praising God and enjoying the favor of all the people. And the Lord added to their number daily those who were being saved. (Acts 2:42-47)

This doesn't describe us. But it does describe many churches around the world in other cultures. The problem is that our modern technological culture has ruined our sense of community, both secular and religious. We are driven by our careers, our 9-to-5 schedules, that make a vital church community virtually impossible. I can't imagine how we can begin to address this problem until we dismantle our modern lifestyle that has forced us away from the life of the church.

There's a sinister aspect to our present state of affairs. It's a military maxim that the enemy can defeat us easily if we drift apart from each other. "Divide and conquer." If we don't assemble together, pool our resources, and come under one command-and-control structure, and move in unison, we will be destroyed easily. All army commanders understand this principle. It's a shame, however, that so few churches understand this.

In fact, it's not just the army that understands this. People will not hesitate to throw themselves into their jobs, their social clubs, and their political causes, with the necessary camaraderie and zeal that it takes to do the job. Yet for some strange reason they fail to see the need for this unity and zeal in the church. It's positively disheartening to see them deliberately hurt and destroy the lives of those they profess to love in the church. The church is often a fierce battleground between opposing wills. Pride, lust, politics, greed, and a host of other motives seem to take first priority in church members' hearts instead of the Mission. As a result, we separate from each other, we lose the battle, and many of us don't achieve the Mission.

One thing that a church has to understand and take to heart is that we can't accomplish this Mission on an individual basis. We are not called to be loners. God has made us a Family – because only in unity of spirit and purpose will we achieve our goals.

One of the most fundamental changes that happened to us when we became believers was when God made us *one with Christ*. This single idea makes possible our salvation, the righteousness that the Law expects of us, our relationship to God the Father, and our hope of eternal life in Heaven. It's a profound mystery and yet very real and necessary for the believer.

> ... the mystery that has been kept hidden for ages and generations, but is now disclosed to the saints. To them God has chosen to make known among the Gentiles the glorious riches of this mystery, which is Christ in you, the hope of glory. (Colossians 1:26-27)

In fact, all believers make up the entire Body of Christ – again a mystery, but it explains why the same life is in us all.

> Just as each of us has one body with many members, and these members do not all have the same function, so in

Christ we who are many form one body, and each member belongs to all the others. (Romans 12:4-5)

Nobody can explain how it happens, but the entire number of Christians down through the ages, and across the world, form one Body that lives by the Spirit of Christ. He is the Head, and we are the "cells," as it were, and the parts of the Body that make a whole. None of us is unnecessary to the body, and every one of us is needed for its function and well-being.

The idea is that we live *together*; if we pull away, we die, just as a part of your physical body will die if it's cut off from the rest. We need what the rest of the body provides for us, and they need us.

We already saw the role of spiritual gifts in the church. Each part of the body is gifted for the benefit of the whole body; we each rely on one another for what we ourselves can't do. This is the way the Lord changes us all; being in close proximity to the power and wisdom of Heaven, through our brothers and sisters, strengthens and guides us all.

The image of the church being the Body of Christ is useful to teach us some vital principles of the life and function of the church. But it's not the only image we can use. The Bible also calls us the **family** of God in order to teach us about other principles of church life.

This passage in Matthew shows us what Jesus thinks of the family of God – it was more important to him than his earthly family.

> While Jesus was still talking to the crowd, his mother and brothers stood outside, wanting to speak to him. Someone told him, "Your mother and brothers are standing outside, wanting to speak to you." He replied to him, "Who is my mother, and who are my brothers?" Pointing to his disciples, he said, "Here are my mother and my brothers. For whoever does the will of my Father in Heaven is my brother and sister and mother." (Matthew 12:49-50)

The reason he feels this way is because he's putting together a new family, one that will outlast the destruction of this world and live on in Heaven. Earthly families don't often stick together on spiritual matters. The church, however, is made up of people who are vitally concerned with the state of their souls and how to go to Heaven. They are there to work on *this* project. And since Jesus was primarily in this world for that one reason, he of course focuses his attention, affection and work on those saints who want to go with him.

> Both the one who makes men holy and those who are made holy are of the same family. So Jesus is not ashamed to call them brothers. He says, "I will declare your name to my brothers; in the presence of the congregation I will sing your praises." And again, "I will put my trust in him." And again he says, "Here am I, and the children God has given me." Since the children have flesh and blood, he too shared in their humanity so that by his death he might destroy him who holds the power of death – that is, the devil – and free those who all their lives were held in slavery by their fear of death. (Hebrews 2:11-15)

Like it or not, Jesus has little time for anybody else. "I was sent only to the lost sheep of Israel." (Matthew 15:24) He loves his brothers and sisters; he works day and night for their benefit; he has poured out his life for them. They are his family, children born of his Spirit by the will of God.

> Yet to all who received him, to those who believed in his name, he gave the right to become children of God – children born not of natural descent, nor of human decision or a husband's will, but born of God. (John 1:12-13)

Are these Christians so much different from the rest of humanity that they warrant his complete attention and love? They are more different than you can know! They are members of a new race of man. Whereas our present world is populated with children of Adam – and rebellious and cursed as a result of that ancestry – the people of God have been created along new lines. They are designed to know and love and serve the spiritual God *without fail*, forever.

> So it is written: "The first man Adam became a living being"; the last Adam, a life-giving spirit. The spiritual did not come first, but the natural, and after that the spiritual.

The first man was of the dust of the earth, the second man from Heaven. As was the earthly man, so are those who are of the earth; and as is the man from Heaven, so also are those who are of Heaven. And just as we have borne the likeness of the earthly man, so shall we bear the likeness of the man from Heaven. (1 Corinthians 15:45-49)

We can see this "new man" in Jesus himself, who was the pioneer, the forerunner, of the new race. We also see this "new man" in the life of the church, as the Spirit of Christ conforms us into Christ's image. As the Spirit works among the church members, life pours out among us and re-creates each of us into the "new man."

His purpose was to create in himself one new man out of the two, thus making peace, and in this one body to reconcile both of them to God through the cross, by which he put to death their hostility. He came and preached peace to you who were far away and peace to those who were near. For through him we both have access to the Father by one Spirit. Consequently, you are no longer foreigners and aliens, but fellow citizens with God's people and members of God's household. (Ephesians 2:15-19)

This brings up another important point. The Jews think that they are automatically deserving of Heaven since they are physically descended from Abraham; they are mistaken about this. But so are a lot of people in church mistaken about the idea of "family." We have to distinguish between earthly families and God's spiritual family. God doesn't draw the line in the same places that we want to see them. The Jews erred in considering genetic descent as a qualification; so do modern Christians, it seems.

Jesus knew that many people would make the mistake of putting their earthly families above the church. He spoke to this issue on many occasions. For example, here is what he expects from earthly families.

For I have come to turn 'a man against his father, a daughter against her mother, a daughter-in-law against her

mother-in-law – a man's enemies will be the members of
his own household.' (Matthew 10:35-36)

As far as he was concerned, he sees that we will encounter the most
problems with our own families. As we struggle to make our way
toward Heaven, our families will often turn out to be our bitterest
enemies. Jesus was pretty skeptical about how useful our families are
going to be on our spiritual journey. In fact, there are about ten places
in the Gospels where Jesus talks about our families, and none of them
are positive. He was either indifferent about the subject, or downright
skeptical. He sees no help from that quarter.

He also knows our hearts. When it comes time to choose between
family and church, we will almost always choose the family. That's a
mistake. Our earthly families will rarely follow us to Heaven; the
church family, however, is going to be there waiting for us. How
willing are we to follow our brothers and sisters in the faith when our
families demand that we turn aside and spend our energies on them
alone? What will we do when our families demand that we adhere to
their values, when Heaven calls from a different direction? There will
be many faced with that dilemma, and Jesus takes a dim view of those
who turn away from the needs of the church for the sake of their
families.

> Anyone who loves his father or mother more than me is
> not worthy of me; anyone who loves his son or daughter
> more than me is not worthy of me; and anyone who does
> not take his cross and follow me is not worthy of me.
> (Matthew 10:37-38)

It's not that Jesus thinks ill of our families; it's just that he knows
that, for the most part, they won't share your new spiritual values. As
much as you want them to join you in church life, they rarely will.
Most families will divide over this issue of Christianity; you've no
doubt seen it already and know that it's true. It's sad, and it ought not
to be, but it's a fact. Those churches nowadays that try to build a
"family-oriented ministry" didn't get their ideas, nor their optimism
that such a thing will work, from Jesus.

So the Lord refuses to draw the line of God's family around our earthly families. The church is our new family now, and like John Bunyan's Pilgrim, you must go with the church even if your family won't follow you. Here in the church you will find like-minded pilgrims on their way to Heaven. They will care about your spiritual life and are willing to help you on your journey. They have the resources and the calling to help you. They care about your soul in a way that no other earthly institution does.

Your brothers and sisters in church share your spiritual characteristics. They have the same faith that you have, the same Spirit, the same hope of Heaven; they deal with the same spiritual treasures that you value; they have seen the same spiritual Kingdom that you have seen; they are growing the same spiritual fruit in their lives that you are growing. You have much more in common with these people than you have even with your physical family. You are all being groomed and prepared for a new life in Heaven; whereas this world, with all its associations and relationships, is doomed to be destroyed.

In fact, you can run across a believer in any part of the world and discover this mystical unity of purpose and life. You may be citizens of different countries, and disagree violently on political or cultural issues. But if you are both Christians, you walk on a higher plane than the petty differences of this world. You are both destined to live with God. You will find many things in common that show the hand of Christ forming and preparing you for God's world. So, we can't predict how or where God will draw that line that separates his family from the rest of the world, but we will know it when we meet someone inside that line – they will be part of the church. We won't find such kindred spirits in any other earthly relationship.

Love for the family

Now that we've explored the principle of the family of God, we need to examine what that will look like on the church level. What does it mean that a Christian is a part of the family of God?

Let me say first that a church will never work unless both the leadership and the membership are agreed, and determined, about this point. *We are brothers and sisters.* We are not individuals who can live without each other. God put us together in profound wisdom; he made it possible for us to achieve our Mission as a family, not by ourselves.

Of course it's also true that we can't separate from each other over any little problem or whim. Just as physical family members can't deny their relationship, despite problems, so the members of God's household can't deny their relationships. In other words, if you refuse to work out problems and leave the church "offended" with someone, you are only postponing the issue, not solving it. God is going to force you to come back to this problem and deal with it sometime, somewhere. The secret is that it's easier to take care of this the first time around, not the second. Leaving your brothers over some trivial issue only causes even more hurt and suffering that has to be addressed. Then you will have that new crime to answer for as well as the original problem.

The spiritual skill that makes the family work is love. That's why the subject of love is so prevalent in the Bible.

> My command is this: Love each other as I have loved
> you. Greater love has no one than this, that he lay down his
> life for his friends. (John 15:12-13)

Here is the command *and* the definition. We must love each other as Jesus loves us. Spend some time on that idea for a while! To head off any wrong notions on what "love" might mean, Jesus tells us: we must give until it hurts; we must make sure our brother has what he needs, even if it means we have to go without; we must put ourselves out of the picture so that our brother can get into it; we must "consider others better than ourselves." (Philippians 2:3) We must put aside our pride and bear with our brother's immaturity. We must spend time and energy for our brother's benefit.

Now most people in church today don't love like this. How do I know? Simply because we don't even know our brother and his circumstances! How can we *love* him if we're not even close enough to him to know what he needs? And how can we *love* him if we are so ready to declare war against him over trivial matters?

> This is how we know who the children of God are and who the children of the devil are: Anyone who does not do what is right is not a child of God; nor is anyone who does not love his brother. (1 John 3:10)

> If anyone has material possessions and sees his brother in need but has no pity on him, how can the love of God be in him? (1 John 3:17)

> If anyone says, "I love God," yet hates his brother, he is a *liar*. For anyone who does not love his brother, whom he has seen, cannot love God, whom he has not seen. And he has given us this command: Whoever loves God must also love his brother. (1 John 4:20-21)

John obviously feels very strongly about this matter. He has seen a lot of people claim to love their brother and yet their claim was empty. When power or money come to the table, we find out who really loves who! As far as he is concerned, there are a lot of fake "Christians" in today's church who don't love anybody but themselves. They are lying about their "faith."

We might object to such strong language, but John presses his point home and makes it simple for us to understand: they are L...I...A...R...S. People who are only out for themselves, who willingly hurt the sheep to get ahead, who despise authority – such people, as Jude tells us, are a blemish on the church and should not be tolerated any more than they would tolerate Satan himself among them.

> These men are blemishes at your love feasts, eating with you without the slightest qualm – shepherds who feed only themselves. They are clouds without rain, blown along by the wind; autumn trees, without fruit and uprooted – twice dead. They are wild waves of the sea, foaming up their shame; wandering stars, for whom blackest darkness has been reserved forever. Enoch, the seventh from Adam, prophesied about these men: "See, the Lord is coming with thousands upon thousands of his holy ones to judge everyone, and to convict all the ungodly of all the ungodly

acts they have done in the ungodly way, and of all the harsh words ungodly sinners have spoken against him." These men are grumblers and faultfinders; they follow their own evil desires; they boast about themselves and flatter others for their own advantage. (Jude 12-16)

The church can't work if it's filled with a lot of self-seeking, self-serving, proud, rebellious troublemakers who will stop at nothing (including hurting others) to get what they want.

Yet your church can survive, even with all sorts of problems, as long as everyone genuinely loves each other.

Above all, love each other deeply, because love covers over a multitude of sins. Offer hospitality to one another without grumbling. Each one should use whatever gift he has received to serve others, faithfully administering God's grace in its various forms. (1 Peter 4:8-10)

That love will work to *solve* the problems, not generate new ones. That love will bring everyone along in the Mission, and not leave anybody behind. That love will put others first, and not compete against them. As you can see, the gift of love helps each person achieve his goal, because he has so many people at hand who are willing and able to help him get there.

How does it work? Well, we can again use the early church as an example. We've already seen that their church did these things:

- They devoted themselves:

    to the Apostles' teaching,

    to fellowship,

    to breaking bread together,

    to prayer.

- They spent time together.
- They had everything in common.

- They sold their possessions and gave the proceeds to their needy.

- They met every day in the Temple courts.

- They met in their homes and ate together.

In other words, they were free with what they owned, and they liked being around each other – a lot. We are also told, in Acts 4, that there were no needy persons among them.

Priesthood

Another aspect of the church that makes it work is that everyone is doing their job for the sake of others. Jesus has given us spiritual resources to help the church achieve its Mission. They are called the spiritual gifts of the church, and they are given by the Spirit himself. Furthermore, though we often call any ability a "gift" even in the church, only the ones that the Word specifies as a gift qualify.

A spiritual gift is a God-given ability to help others see Christ more clearly and draw closer to him in faith. And that is precisely what is needed. Christ is our life; he's our salvation; he is the wisdom and power of God. Drawing close to him is achieving our goal of living with God in sinless perfection. So, if someone else can help me do that – well, that's where the gifts come in.

The Old Testament teaches us about the functions and roles of the priests in Israel. They provided a critical role in the life of God's people. Interestingly, in the New Testament we learn that we *all* have become priests in God's house.

> You also, like living stones, are being built into a spiritual house to be a holy priesthood, offering spiritual sacrifices acceptable to God through Jesus Christ. (1 Peter 2:5)

> But you are a chosen people, a royal priesthood, a holy nation, a people belonging to God, that you may declare the

praises of him who called you out of darkness into his
wonderful light. (1 Peter 2:9)

> To him who loves us and has freed us from our sins by
> his blood, and has made us to be a kingdom and priests to
> serve his God and Father – to him be glory and power for
> ever and ever! (Revelation 1:5-6)

This means, then, that we now have an obligation to minister to
others, just as the Old Testament priests did. We are in the position of
bringing the blessing of the presence and treasures of God to our
brothers and sisters in need. The result of this faithful work among us,
on the part of us all, is the living Temple where God intends to live
forever.

> In him the whole building is joined together and rises to
> become a holy Temple in the Lord. And in him you too are
> being built together to become a dwelling in which God
> lives by his Spirit. (Ephesians 2:21-22)

One of the Covenant promises that God made to Abraham was that
he would make Abraham and his family into a "great nation." (Genesis
12:2) Abraham soon found out that this meant a world-wide family,
across all cultures and races, from his day to the end of the world. The
Church shares the family trait of Abraham's faith, and inherits the
blessings of the Covenant from their father Abraham.

> I say to you that many will come from the east and the
> west, and will take their places at the feast with Abraham,
> Isaac and Jacob in the kingdom of Heaven. (Matthew 8:11)

One of the benefits of being part of the family of God is that we are
showered with the blessings of Heaven by means of the spiritual gifts
that the Holy Spirit gives each family member. Do you know how God
originally designed the human race to work? Each person had a part of
the mind of God, knowing enough of the will of God to carry out his or
her responsibilities to build and maintain God's Kingdom on earth.
Nobody had all wisdom (except God!) and nobody had all the

responsibilities on his shoulders. We were all to do our part, and the result would be peace and prosperity.

The Spirit brings us back to that original idea by distributing gifts to each member of the church for the benefit of the whole.

> But to each one of us grace has been given as Christ apportioned it. This is why it says: "When he ascended on high, he led captives in his train and gave gifts to men." ... It was he who gave some to be Apostles, some to be Prophets, some to be evangelists, and some to be pastors and teachers, to prepare God's people for works of service, so that the body of Christ may be built up until we all reach unity in the faith and in the knowledge of the Son of God and become mature, attaining to the whole measure of the fullness of Christ. (Ephesians 4:7-8,11-13)

The gifts of the Spirit enable a person to make God real to another person. Through the ministry of someone's gift, we sense the presence, the truth, the power, the discipline, the love, the guidance, the faithfulness, and the wisdom of God among us. We are priests working for each other's benefit by bringing our brothers' and sisters' needs to the throne of grace, and bringing the resources of that throne back to our brothers and sisters in need.

> You are worthy to take the scroll and to open its seals, because you were slain, and with your blood you purchased men for God from every tribe and language and people and nation. You have made them to be a kingdom and priests to serve our God, and they will reign on the earth. (Revelation 5:9-10)

When we all do our part, and accept the ministry of others as from God, then the church works. Paul breathed a sigh of relief that the Thessalonians saw this truth in his ministry.

> And we also thank God continually because, when you received the Word of God, which you heard from us, you accepted it not as the word of men, but as it actually is, the

Word of God, which is at work in you who believe. (1 Thessalonians 2:13)

Even discipline is from God, and we make a terrible mistake when we don't accept it from the hands of those God sent to deliver it to us. It's meant to correct us in our journey toward Heaven; the wise will see that.

> He who listens to a life-giving rebuke will be at home among the wise. He who ignores discipline despises himself, but whoever heeds correction gains understanding. (Proverbs 15:31-32)

Change

I hope you realize that, in order to be of such help to each other, our natures have to change. This too is an area where we are sadly lacking in today's churches. Even in conservative churches, new members are welcomed with open arms – but then their growth comes to a complete halt. Everyone assumes two things: first, that they don't need much more than what they received at conversion to be good Christians. Second, anything that they manage to get in addition to that, they will have to get it on their own. There's certainly no training or rigorous program in place to get them to maturity.

The result is that we still have a lot of nasty character traits about us that too often show themselves in difficult church circumstances. The sins of the flesh are simmering below the surface and nobody is working on them, or even admitting their presence.

> The acts of the sinful nature are obvious: sexual immorality, impurity and debauchery; idolatry and witchcraft; hatred, discord, jealousy, fits of rage, selfish ambition, dissensions, factions and envy; drunkenness, orgies, and the like. I warn you, as I did before, that those who live like this will not inherit the kingdom of God. (Galatians 5:19-21)

Probably every church has its horror stories of church splits, arguments and fights, hostile board meetings, and simmering feuds.

And that's just one aspect of the sinful flesh. There is adultery and immorality, greed and corruption, lying and deceiving, politicking, apathy and laziness going on in churches – this sordid list describes the church as well as the world. When things like these come up, everyone wonders how it could happen in a *church!* The fact is that nobody addressed this spiritual reality, neither the pulpit nor the pew. Everyone ignored it, thinking that if nobody talked about it, then maybe it would all go away when they got converted. It didn't go away, and it never will, as long as people don't directly confront the enemy and systematically destroy it before it destroys them.

Just to get along with each other, let alone do something good for one another, we have to crucify this junk in our hearts and replace it with the fruit of the Spirit.

> But the fruit of the Spirit is love, joy, peace, patience, kindness, goodness, faithfulness, gentleness and self-control. Against such things there is no law. Those who belong to Christ Jesus have crucified the sinful nature with its passions and desires. (Galatians 5:22-24)

Someone who lives like this is a *nice person.* They will be a great source of help toward others. You aren't going to have any problems out of them. Fill a church with people like this, and you have a church with a Mission! Everyone will be busy ministering to the needs of others.

People have often wished that life could be a utopia – a perfect world. Many thinkers have come up with schemes to create that kind of a world. But they are all doomed to fail, because man can't make such a world come about.

But Christ can – and will. The world he is creating is not only going to be perfect, but it's going to last forever in its perfection. In fact, the church is the foretaste of that perfect world that is coming. *It is the only place on earth where such things can happen.* The most strict government on earth can only pass laws and hope to terrify people into submission. The Lord, however, puts his Spirit in the hearts of his people and changes them from the inside out. He makes them *want* to be righteous and holy.

The church alone has the resources to make this happen. Notice in the following passage that Paul assumes that they will be like Christ *if* they have certain spiritual realities in operation.

> If you have any encouragement from being united with Christ, if any comfort from his love, if any fellowship with the Spirit, if any tenderness and compassion, then make my joy complete by being like-minded, having the same love, being one in spirit and purpose. Do nothing out of selfish ambition or vain conceit, but in humility consider others better than yourselves. Each of you should look not only to your own interests, but also to the interests of others. Your attitude should be the same as that of Christ Jesus. (Philippians 2:1-5)

The church that you are in could be laboring under all sorts of difficulties; however, if the members are truly united with Christ and have his Spirit in them, there is hope. They will see each other as family, and they will put themselves out for the benefit of each other. To them, the church is their life. As the Psalmist said, "God sets the lonely in families." (Psalm 68:6) The church is a garden where our fruit will grow. The church is a household, where the family can grow and mature. In order to succeed, however, the church has to be bound together as a family and care for each other.

If this doesn't happen in the church, it's certainly not going to happen anywhere else. Because the world doesn't care at all about you. In the world, people gravitate toward the young, the strong, the rich, and the beautiful. In the church, though, we are to gravitate toward the lowly, the forsaken, the despised of the world – those in need. Our family are those who are "hungering and thirsting after righteousness." We Christians are the only ones who will care about them, because we know what it's like for someone to love us.

> But God demonstrates his own love for us in this: While we were still sinners, Christ died for us. (Romans 5:8)

When things go wrong

What are the fail-safes that the Lord has given the church as it follows human leadership?

- *According to the Word* (*Acts 17:11*) – The Berean church even checked up on the Apostle Paul by comparing what he taught them against the Word of God. Remember that Jesus rules over us through his Word. That Word is open to anybody, from the least to the greatest. It's not the private property of the leaders of the church – as the Roman Catholics attempted to impose during the Middle Ages. Anybody with the Spirit of Christ leading him can read the Bible for himself and see what it says. If a teacher or preacher is teaching a doctrine or living a life that is directly contrary to the Word (if he is, others besides yourself will see it too – be careful of being a lone ranger with zeal and no knowledge!) then he needs to be confronted and dealt with. The ultimate authority in the church is the Lord and his Word, not the human leadership.

- *Two or three witnesses* (*1 Timothy 5:19*) – The leader of a church is a natural target for discontented troublemakers; he shouldn't be subjected to false accusations from members who don't like the way things are going. However, if a leader really has done something that needs correcting, there should be a few witnesses (more than one, so that no lone wolf can make trouble for the church) who can verify that there really is something wrong with this elder. If there was something done or said that was injurious to the flock, the witnesses will have a clear, unified testimony that will easily convince the whole assembly. Rebuking an elder is a serious matter and should be done with care and deliberation. There is proper protocol and procedure for this; it's not a time for mob rule or midnight lynchings!

- *Subject to the prophets* (*1 Corinthians 14:32*) – Those who bring the Word of God to the sheep are not free to make things up. How many leaders have felt free to add a little fire to the text to make themselves more powerful and wise in the eyes of the ignorant! Remember that there are other saints in the assembly that have the same spirit of discernment to the true meaning of the Word as he does. If that's really what the text says, they will agree with him. But if it isn't saying that at all, they are duty bound to disagree and correct him.

- *As I follow Christ* (*1 Corinthians 11:1*) – Paul was filled with the reality of his calling as an Apostle; he knew the Lord had assigned him the task of taking the Gospel to the Gentiles and start building churches. His back was covered by the Lord's own appointment. Still, he knew that he was just a man, subject to weakness and ignorance as is any man. So he counseled his students to take his ministry seriously – in so far as he himself followed Christ and followed his example. Who can argue with that? If Christ commanded us to live a certain way, then we are bound to live that way also, as the leaders show us how. If this is what Christ said, then church members are obligated to believe it no matter who teaches it to them. The leaders' authority comes from having Christ's mantle put upon themselves, by his authority, and leading by his divine example.

- *Let the spirit convict* (*Philippians 3:15-16*) – Church members are obligated to learn and do what their leaders teach them. Their dependence on the leaders makes them vulnerable. It's that childlike dependence that makes some men giddy with power and it tempts them to overstep their bounds. They go beyond their calling and demand that "their" people follow their instructions exactly, immediately, if they want their approval. Leaders, however, can't police people's thoughts, their actions during the day, or their practices in the privacy of their homes. We can tell them what the Lord expects of them, but we can't change their hearts to want to live that way. As leaders we are responsible to show them the way, but we can't make them walk in it. Only the Spirit of God can change a sinner's heart to love God and want to obey him. *There* is the wisdom of leadership – to know where man's responsibilities end and where the Lord's work begins.

- *The Bride of Christ* (*Ephesians 5:25-27*) – The last point relates to this one. The church leaders don't own the church, and the members don't belong to the leaders. This is not man's kingdom. Christ bought these people with his own blood. They belong to him alone. The leaders are appointed as under-shepherds; they are only delivering a message from the Bridegroom. Once that message is delivered, it's their duty to step out of the way and let Christ deal with his Bride as he wishes. The practical side of this is seen in how church leaders follow up on their ministries. If they are putting themselves in Christ's place, they will follow people home and beat the sheep until people do what they want from them. But if they consider themselves only to be messengers from the Lord, they will leave obedience and sanctification in Christ's hands and timing. Instead of beating the sheep, they pray for them, counsel them, and keep teaching them with the hope that someday the Spirit will change their hearts.

- *The three stages of Matthew 18* – This well-known passage gives us a clear, simple procedure for dealing with any trouble maker in the church, whether he be member or leader. First, the brother or sister living in sin is approached by the person he offended. If he won't listen, then the matter goes to a few others – including, hopefully, some witnesses who can prove the point. At some point the leaders in the church should be included to make sure that this is really a spiritual problem, and it isn't just a minor spat or somebody taking unnecessary offense with someone else. Then if the offender won't listen, take it to the church level. At this point, the whole church makes it plain to the offender that this kind of behavior is injurious to the peace of the church and will not be tolerated. This procedure is both fair and merciful and, if done in the Spirit of Christ, should take care of any problem that would arise in the church – including dealing with wayward leaders.

A well-disciplined Church

Let's go back to the war model again and look at the "militant church."

When one army comes against another, we will be able to tell if it's been training for battle, just by the way it handles itself on the battlefield. Let's say that Army B (the typical church) launches an attack on its enemy.

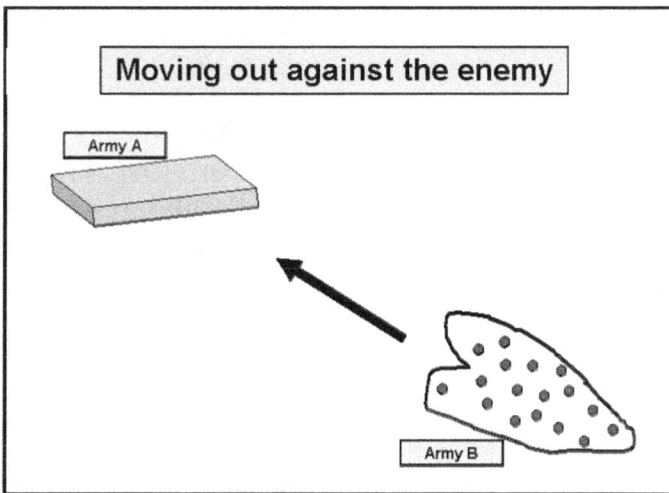

A mob attacks a disciplined enemy

Army B doesn't know what it's doing. It hasn't been training for battle. It suddenly ran across the enemy in the field; and even though there's been no formal training and nobody is really leading this mob, everyone thinks that they can win the battle. Let's see what actually happens.

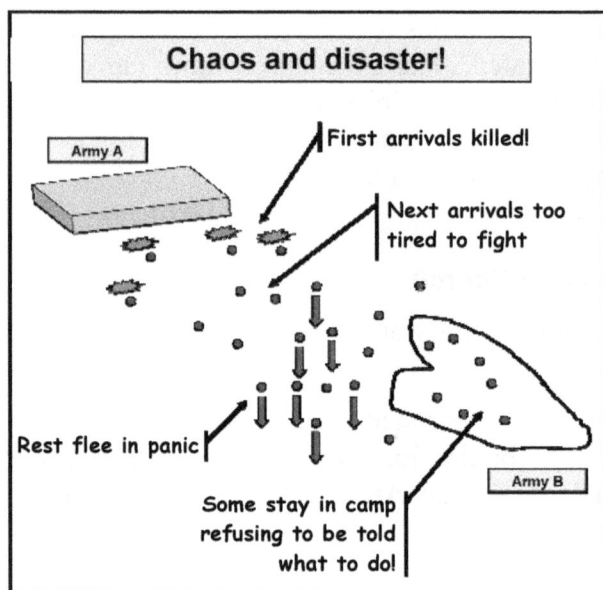

Chaos and disaster!

Army A

First arrivals killed!

Next arrivals too tired to fight

Rest flee in panic

Some stay in camp refusing to be told what to do!

Army B

The mob loses the battle

When the fighting begins, we can see proofs of the lack of leadership, training and foresight. A few enterprising troops run across the field in their zeal and energy, and are easily cut down since they have no support around them. The slower troops behind them, as they are crossing the field, come too late and are too tired to give battle. The later ones see the slaughter ahead of them and turn and run away out of fear. There are even a few of the mob who refused to go out and fight; they are still back in camp rebelling against the whole idea!

Army A wins this battle easily, because Army B didn't know what it was doing. It wasn't even a close contest.

Now let's say that Army B learned its lesson (if there were any troops left after the fight!). They appointed experienced leaders who trained the troops day and night. Everyone learned their role in battle, how to use their equipment, and what to do in tough situations. They learned how to march in step and unison. They have drilled so much that, even in the middle of bombs, bullets and bayonet charges, they keep their cool and do what they were trained to do.

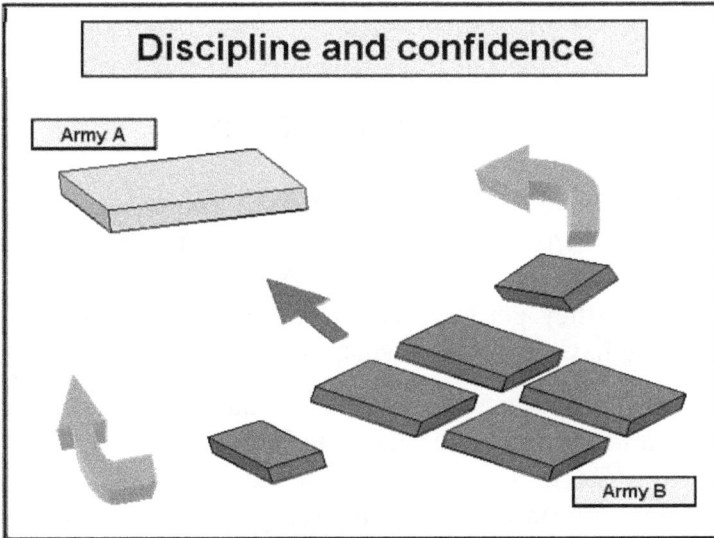

A well-disciplined army about to win

You can tell just by looking at how Army B approaches its enemy that it is well-trained, disciplined, and confident. The difference is a beautiful thing to behold. Army A is about to be surrounded and annihilated!

Would to God that churches would do this simple thing and get ready for war. People are going to be showing up on the church's doorstep in times of disaster, so churches have to come up with a plan for delivering these people from their enemies and getting them out of this world and into Heaven. These are difficult times, and we do not have the leisure to play games anymore. It's time to get the church ready to perform its Mission.

General Discipline

Some people have their wits about them. You can tell – there's just something about them that makes them a survivor. Others, however ... you shake your head over them; they seemed doomed to fail. You just know that, when they get in trouble over their heads, they're going to fall apart. They have no idea of what's going on around them.

Unfortunately not every Christian is a survivor. I've seen it over and over again: someone who claims to be a Christian collapses under the weight of trials, losses, setbacks, alienation, and persecution. They cry, they freeze up and can't do anything, they blame God or other people for what's happening to them. No one can do much for them, either; how can you impart years of training, wisdom and know-how to someone who hasn't been listening? How can you turn the clock back and equip them when they're already lying on the battlefield wounded? It's too late to do much for them at that point. We just have another casualty on our hands to deal with. The shame is that it didn't have to be this way.

One of the indicators, of course, that a person is a survivor is that they're paying attention to the training ahead of time. It's as if they're in a classroom: they are taking notes, they are practicing the material, they are disciplining themselves for future trials. The slackers, in the meantime, are goofing off in class. It works the same way as in public school: the studious types are headed for good jobs and successful lives; the lazy, defiant ones are doomed to be one of society's burdens and liabilities, because they won't even be able to take care of themselves, let alone be a positive influence on others. We feel sorry for these people when they get in trouble, but the truth is that they brought this on themselves; now the rest of us have to pay their bills.

Jesus said that "in this world, you will have trouble." (John 16:33) Instead of ignoring him, *every Christian has the opportunity and duty to prepare for those trials*. How can any of us say that we can't be prepared? We have all the resources of Heaven at our disposal; we have the roadmap in the Bible that gets us through a dark world; we have opportunities for training and drilling so that we can get good at our faith; we have Jesus himself empowering us, filling us, strengthening us through his Spirit. We can't lose! The only way we can possibly fail at this Mission is if we aren't paying any attention to it. Millions of people in the past have taken this Heavenly course of instruction and passed their test; it doesn't require genius or wealth or an aristocratic position in society. The lowliest, the poorest, and the weakest have taken the "yoke of Christ" upon themselves and succeeded in the fiercest of trials.

What it takes is character, and you can learn it. Not everyone is born with a survivor's character; but it can be acquired over time, if you persevere in it. For some of us it takes a *long* time, whereas others learn quickly. No matter – God oversees your education and progress, and he won't let you go through more than you can handle. If we ever feel that we are in over our heads, it's only because God has already put the resources that we need at our disposal and we aren't paying attention to him. Then he'll let us suffer a while until we start listening again and get back into the program.

Hardship and trials

God doesn't pave the way to Heaven with a golden road. Jesus himself pioneered the way, and it was anything but a joy-ride. The way to God involves hardship, trial, privation and suffering.

> I am the way and the truth and the life. No one comes to the Father except through me. (John 14:6)

> If anyone would come after me, he must deny himself and take up his cross daily and follow me. For whoever wants to save his life will lose it, but whoever loses his life for me will save it. What good is it for a man to gain the whole world, and yet lose or forfeit his very self? (Luke 9:23-25)

> If the world hates you, keep in mind that it hated me first. If you belonged to the world, it would love you as its own. As it is, you do not belong to the world, but I have

chosen you out of the world. That is why the world hates you. Remember the words I spoke to you: "No servant is greater than his master." If they persecuted me, they will persecute you also. (John 15:18-20)

Rather, as servants of God we commend ourselves in every way: in great endurance; in troubles, hardships and distresses; in beatings, imprisonments and riots; in hard work, sleepless nights and hunger; in purity, understanding, patience and kindness; in the Holy Spirit and in sincere love; in truthful speech and in the power of God; with weapons of righteousness in the right hand and in the left; through glory and dishonor, bad report and good report; genuine, yet regarded as impostors; known, yet regarded as unknown; dying, and yet we live on; beaten, and yet not killed; sorrowful, yet always rejoicing; poor, yet making many rich; having nothing, and yet possessing everything. (2 Corinthians 6:4-10)

This doesn't look appealing at all! Remember, the reason that Christianity is not smooth sailing is that you have very determined enemies who are desperately trying to keep you from achieving your Mission. If it weren't for them, things would be a lot easier. I suppose it depends on how badly you want to be with God. If you don't care, you won't fight; if you *love* God, however, and at least *try*, you'll find that he's working from his end to get you there. He won't leave you here alone. That's very encouraging.

You may as well know up front what's in store for you.

- **Persecution** – People aren't going to like your Christianity. You remind them of God, and they don't want to think about God. They're going to be very unjust and underhanded in dealing with you. You will be accused of things that you didn't do; you will find them opposing you when you try to live your faith; they will start vicious rumors about you in the community. Persecution takes many forms, from subtle attitudes to outright loss of life and limb. It's hard to be in a world where almost everyone around you is a potential enemy; you can't share what's on your heart with hardly anybody for fear they will use it to hurt you in return.

- **Long stretches** – The road can be long and weary for a Christian. Though we like to live on a spiritual high all the time, it doesn't work like that. Hard times can last a long time; trials go on and on, longer than we thought possible to endure. The pressure is intense and unrelenting. We need rest, and yet there is none. The goal seems just as far away on the horizon as when we started; it doesn't seem as if we're making any progress at all. We plead with God to do something while day after day stretches out in unbroken hardship. We wonder what God is doing when he doesn't answer us long after the point of no return – what good could he do if we're already broken? Why didn't he send answers when we needed them?

- **Privation** – At times, you will have to do without a lot of things that other people take for granted. You are an "alien and a stranger" in this world. God doesn't feel the necessity to give you what everyone else has. Homes, jobs, health, entertainment and vacations, possessions and wealth, even family and friends – you may have these things, but you may be required to do without them. There will be times when God takes these things away from you! Remember that none of it is a *right*; any good thing in this world is a *gift* from God, and he alone knows best what you need spiritually. It may be that these things will interfere in some way with your spiritual growth and training. God is not going to let anything stand in the way of you achieving your Mission, no matter how badly you may want it.

- **Loneliness** – Being a Christian can be one of the loneliest jobs on earth! Unbelievers don't like to be around you. What hurts worse, some who call themselves "Christians" won't share your zeal and love for God; they'll accuse you of taking this religion business too seriously. Your own family will think that you're strange. God will be leading you down roads of hardship, training, privation and war, and nobody is going to want to go with you. You may end up working on God's program by yourself; it will take a lot of self-discipline, and the willingness and ability to check yourself for progress. People you know probably won't understand a thing about what you're doing!

- **Injustice** – This world is already full of injustice, but what makes it hurt worse is when we are trying our best to please God and follow him and yet everything works against us. As Ecclesiastes puts it, life is so upside down when the righteous get what the wicked deserve and the wicked get what the righteous deserve. Why are the wicked praised and made heroes in our society while Christians are despised and persecuted? Why do the wicked have the best things in life, and the Christians have to suffer loss? Get used to it: in this world there will be no justice. Even when you try to get justice, it never seems to work out. People are always looking out for themselves, and they certainly aren't willing to give you your fair share.

- **Out of our control** – A human being hates being helpless. Unfortunately for Christians, we are often victims instead of rulers. Events go from bad to worse and there's nothing we can do about it. Ours is not a push-button religion; you can't guarantee success and easy times simply by doing the right things. We pray, and yet we don't get answers; we wait, and nothing happens; we obey, yet suffer even more. Things don't make sense to us; why is it that even when we try to do things right, we seem to lose ground anyway?

- **No news** – Another thing we hate is a lack of information. We want to know what's going on around us; we want to hear back from fellow travelers; we want to hear how the battle is going. But this world is a fog, a darkness, a brooding silence typical of a battlefield. We have no light; we hear nothing encouraging but only what tends to discourage us and throw us into despair. Like Elijah, we wonder if we're the only ones around who still believe in God! What is even more disconcerting is when Heaven itself seems silent. Our prayers get no answers; we don't know if God is listening or whether he's planning to do anything at all to help us. Our only hope is in what the Bible says – but it says so many different things! Which part is for us?

These kinds of things can be very discouraging. The good part is that we have been forewarned – and as the saying goes, forewarned is forearmed. We can at least start getting ready *now* to store up resources and wisdom for when those hard times come.

Trials and hardships can be brutal. Nobody is exempt: both young and old, men and women, the wise and the ignorant, the good and the bad, are all open and exposed to this world's harsh realities.

> All share a common destiny – the righteous and the wicked, the good and the bad, the clean and the unclean, those who offer sacrifices and those who do not. As it is with the good man, so with the sinner; as it is with those who take oaths, so with those who are afraid to take them. This is the evil in everything that happens under the sun: The same destiny overtakes all. (Ecclesiastes 9:2-3)

Times of trial, for as much as we don't understand their purpose, serve a *vital* purpose in God's hands. As we've mentioned earlier, fire tests our quality. God is probing our hearts so that we might see whether or not our faith is genuine, or if we are more tied to this world's temptations and ways than we are aware of. He wants us to know how well founded on the truth we really are, or whether we still subscribe to the lies and deceits of the enemy. So he tests us. He would never ask us what we think of ourselves!

> His eyes are on the ways of men; he sees their every step. There is no dark place, no deep shadow, where evildoers can hide. God has no need to examine men further, that they should come before him for judgment. (Job 34:21-23)

> But Jesus would not entrust himself to them, for he knew all men. He did not need man's testimony about man, for he knew what was in a man. (John 2:24-25)

The fire, we learn in 1 Corinthians 3, exposes our foundations. If we've built our hope and our religion on "wood, hay or straw," we will never survive hard times and disasters. We didn't bother to build our lives on the Rock, and now we will have to pay the penalty. If, however, we've been careful to build our lives on the "gold, silver, and costly stones" of Heaven, the storms of life won't be any fun but we *can* weather them successfully.

Besides, the tree that strengthens itself against the weather gets stronger and stronger as a result – which is another purpose that God has for testing us.

Survivor stories

One of the purposes of the Bible stories is to show us these survival principles in action. If those people could do it – and they were flesh and blood, as we are, sinners and helpless without God just as we are – then we have hope that we can make it as well. Their secret is our answer: to rest on God alone, and to keep a light touch on the things of this world.

Paul immediately comes to mind, because we have such an extended story about him throughout the New Testament. It's as if the Lord deliberately raised him up as an example for the rest of us. He was a Christian; and look what a *Christian* had to suffer through for the sake of Christ! Being an Apostle didn't spare him from troubles. He himself catalogs the list of hardships that the Lord required him to endure.

> We do not want you to be uninformed, brothers, about the hardships we suffered in the province of Asia. We were under great pressure, far beyond our ability to endure, so that we despaired even of life. Indeed, in our hearts we felt the sentence of death. But this happened that we might not

rely on ourselves but on God, who raises the dead. (2 Corinthians 1:8)

> I have worked much harder, been in prison more frequently, been flogged more severely, and been exposed to death again and again. Five times I received from the Jews the forty lashes minus one. Three times I was beaten with rods, once I was stoned, three times I was shipwrecked, I spent a night and a day in the open sea, I have been constantly on the move. I have been in danger from rivers, in danger from bandits, in danger from my own countrymen, in danger from Gentiles; in danger in the city, in danger in the country, in danger at sea; and in danger from false brothers. I have labored and toiled and have often gone without sleep; I have known hunger and thirst and have often gone without food; I have been cold and naked. Besides everything else, I face daily the pressure of my concern for all the churches. (2 Corinthians 11:23-28)

Few Christians that I know of have gone through hardships like these! Yet Paul kept going. Not only did he persevere, he kept a *good attitude* about it.

> Therefore we do not lose heart. Though outwardly we are wasting away, yet inwardly we are being renewed day by day. For our light and momentary troubles are achieving for us an eternal glory that far outweighs them all. So we fix our eyes not on what is seen, but on what is unseen. For what is seen is temporary, but what is unseen is eternal. (2 Corinthians 4:16-18)

> Therefore I will boast all the more gladly about my weaknesses, so that Christ's power may rest on me. That is why, for Christ's sake, I delight in weaknesses, in insults, in hardships, in persecutions, in difficulties. For when I am weak, then I am strong. (2 Corinthians 12:9-10)

Many of the New Testament saints considered persecution and hardship to be an *honor*. Paul wrote to the church of Thessalonica to encourage them in their suffering; it was achieving a greater spiritual good in their lives than they were aware of.

> Therefore, among God's churches we boast about your perseverance and faith in all the persecutions and trials you are enduring. All this is evidence that God's judgment is right, and as a result you will be counted worthy of the kingdom of God, for which you are suffering. (2 Thessalonians 1:4-5)

What was of greater importance than their physical comfort and well-being was their *spiritual* standing. Could they remain in Christ no matter what the trial? Though the trial would at times be extreme, the Rock on which they stood was greater than any hardship. "Take heart! I have overcome the world." God was using them as witnesses to his power and wisdom. They were part of a grander project – his Kingdom – and they didn't have time for the lesser affairs of this world. In such times, we don't have the liberty to insist on our rights or our comforts.

The Lord Jesus honors those who willingly undergo hardships for his sake. It's not an easy thing to do, it goes against our natural instincts, and it proves the spiritual strength of a person. First honors go to the saints who persevere in hardships *with joy*. For example, in Hebrews 11, after going through a long list of Old Testament saints who willingly endured trials for God's Name, the author says of them that "the world was not worthy of them." (Hebrews 11:38) Now their names are forever engraved with honor in the Scriptures.

Moses endured forty years of hardships: not only was he himself one of the Israelites who had to wander in the desert all that time, but he also had the unimaginable burden of leading and governing millions of hard-headed, hard-hearted, ignorant rebels who gave him no end of troubles. Still, he persevered to the end, accomplished his task, and got his reward.

The Lord himself picked David to be Israel's king, yet he lived as an outlaw for years in the wilderness while King Saul did everything he could to hunt him down and kill him. The injustice done to David was appalling and was evident to everyone, including Saul's own son. Then when David became king, he had years of trouble on his hands with the rebellious northern tribes who harbored deep resentments against him. But he persevered to the end, pulled the nation together, and got his reward.

Jeremiah entered his ministry already knowing the hardships he was about to face.

> But the LORD said to me, "Do not say, 'I am only a child.' You must go to everyone I send you to and say whatever I command you. Do not be afraid of them, for I am with you and will rescue you," declares the LORD. (Jeremiah 1:7-8)

So did Ezekiel.

> The people to whom I am sending you are obstinate and stubborn. Say to them, 'This is what the Sovereign LORD says.' And whether they listen or fail to listen – for they are a rebellious house – they will know that a prophet has been among them. And you, son of man, do not be afraid of them or their words. Do not be afraid, though briers and thorns are all around you and you live among scorpions. Do not be afraid of what they say or terrified by them, though they are a rebellious house. You must speak my words to them, whether they listen or fail to listen, for they are rebellious. (Ezekiel 2:4-7)

The point is that nobody was exempt from testing. The greatest saints had to suffer along with the "nobodies" that we never hear about. *All* of God's children have to be purged of their sin, their dependence on this world, their waywardness from God's holiness, their fears and failures. Since our strength and life is in God alone, one mustn't make the mistake of thinking that trying to be a "better Christian" will obligate God to back off and make our lives easier as a reward. In fact, he will probably do the opposite: if you're such a stellar performer, he will want to "show you off" to an incredulous world!

> For God, who said, "Let light shine out of darkness," made his light shine in our hearts to give us the light of the

knowledge of the glory of God in the face of Christ. But we have this treasure in jars of clay to show that this all-surpassing power is from God and not from us. We are hard pressed on every side, but not crushed; perplexed, but not in despair; persecuted, but not abandoned; struck down, but not destroyed. We always carry around in our body the death of Jesus, so that the life of Jesus may also be revealed in our body. For we who are alive are always being given over to death for Jesus' sake, so that his life may be revealed in our mortal body. (2 Corinthians 4:6-11)

What will it take to survive?

What did these people have that made them survivors in even the most difficult circumstances? Along with the vital resources that we've already looked at, they had some character traits that made them *hold on* in the storm.

- **Wisdom** – Wisdom is the ability to see the bigger picture. God sees the whole picture of the universe, so his wisdom is profound and infinite. He is surprised by nothing, and he knows "the end from the beginning." We can't see things as he does, but we can sit at his feet and get a glimpse of part of what he sees, which is more than we could ever achieve on our own.

    Wise men crave the wisdom of God. They know that God sees the hearts of men and women; nobody can hide anything from him. They know that God sees the hidden spiritual realities that guide this physical world. They know that God set up roads in this world that lead to him, and the enemy has created roads that lead away from God; only God can tell us the difference.

    We are so caught up in the affairs of our individual lives that we often "can't see the forest for the trees." It helps so much to be lifted up above the immediate circumstances so that we can see the surroundings, the lay of the land, the roads in and out, what is coming ahead and what just happened. This "mountain-top view," as God sees it, is another word for wisdom.

People with wisdom seem to know where they are going in life. They are able to survive when others are struggling in the dark. Circumstances don't surprise them; they are balanced in their emotions; they handle problems better. They know what is important and what isn't.

They weren't necessarily born with this ability; they followed directions just as any of the rest of us could if we were so inclined. They got it by studying, meditating on, and living the truth in the Word of God. The Bible was their life-blood. They started out like anybody else, learning the basics like children; but they kept at it year after year until they grew to be masters of the Book. They learned to think God's thoughts; the spiritual Kingdom of God became more important and real to them over the years. They grew spiritually on the Word.

> Like newborn babies, crave pure spiritual milk, so that by it you may grow up in your salvation, now that you have tasted that the Lord is good. (1 Peter 2:2-3)

Growing in wisdom means that you are becoming more useful to God and to the church. Not only are you more aware of your own need for righteousness and holiness, but you can also work more efficiently to help the rest of the church grow in the same way.

> Anyone who lives on milk, being still an infant, is not acquainted with the teaching about righteousness. But solid food is for the mature, who by constant use have trained themselves to distinguish good from evil. (Hebrews 5:13-14)

A person who has wisdom will keep the course to Heaven and avoid the pitfalls that ruin so many people's lives. He will see the clear road to God.

I keep asking that the God of our Lord Jesus Christ, the glorious Father, may give you the Spirit of wisdom and revelation, so that you may know him better. I pray also that the eyes of your heart may be enlightened in order that you may know the hope to which he has called you, the riches of his glorious inheritance in the saints, and his incomparably great power for us who believe. (Ephesians 1:17-19)

- **Love for God and man** – Jesus called this love the "greatest of the commandments," and for good reason. Love for God and man oils the wheels of life.

    Let love and faithfulness never leave you; bind them around your neck, write them on the tablet of your heart. Then you will win favor and a good name in the sight of God and man. (Proverbs 3:3-4)

Love for God means that you want him alone. God is more important to you than anything else; he alone is good; we need him, more than even food and drink. (Matthew 4:4) We live only to joyfully serve him; we fear to offend him with even our thoughts; our sole aim in life is to bring him glory and praise, because he fully deserves it. We want to be God-centered.

That means that we study how to please him. We extend ourselves to the utmost to know him and serve him. We feel the same way about God that Paul felt.

    I want to know Christ and the power of his resurrection and the fellowship of sharing in his sufferings, becoming like him in his death, and so, somehow, to attain to the resurrection from the dead. Not that I have already obtained all this, or have already been made perfect, but I press on to take hold of that for which Christ Jesus took hold of me. Brothers, I do not consider myself yet to have taken hold of it. But one thing I do: Forgetting what is behind and straining toward what is ahead, I press on toward the goal to win the prize for which God has called me Heavenward in Christ Jesus. (Philippians 3:10-14)

This kind of love will cost you, of course, because you will have to set aside everything in this world that used to attract you. That's why the word "love" in Greek is *agape* (ἀγάπη), the kind of love that sacrifices self for someone else. That's of little concern to the one who loves God, though, because he's getting something far better in God than what he had to give up.

And everyone who has left houses or brothers or sisters or father or mother or children or fields for my sake will receive a hundred times as much and will inherit eternal life. (Matthew 19:29)

Consider, too, what God gave up to have you – his own Son! "This is how we know what love is: Jesus Christ laid down his life for us." (1 John 3:16) A person who loves God like this is guaranteed success; God will never leave or forsake his own child.

And if you want to get along with your neighbor, love goes a long way. How can you hate someone when they love you in return? Even if someone persecutes you, being gentle and slow to anger with them, and quick to forgive them, will often defuse a potential war.

A gentle answer turns away wrath, but a harsh word stirs up anger. (Proverbs 15:1)

But I tell you, Do not resist an evil person. If someone strikes you on the right cheek, turn to him the other also. And if someone wants to sue you and take your tunic, let him have your cloak as well.

If someone forces you to go one mile, go with him two miles. (Matthew 5:39-41)

Jesus had many interesting insights on how to treat your neighbor. If we all lived like that, there would be a lot less trouble in this world! Paul, too, has counsel for us here.

Do nothing out of selfish ambition or vain conceit, but in humility consider others better than yourselves. Each of you should look not only to your own interests, but also to the interests of others. (Philippians 2:3-4)

The church is where we have the best chance to put our love into action, since we are all brothers and sisters in Christ; we're supposed to love each other! The idea is that these people love us, and they're willing to go the extra mile to help us grow spiritually. So even if we have trouble loving our neighbor – even if we are still rough around the edges, so to speak – fellow Christians will know how to forbear and pray for us.

Above all, love each other deeply, because love covers over a multitude of sins. (1 Peter 4:8)

- **Priorities** – We get so caught up in the affairs of daily life that we forget the really big issues. There's nothing wrong with making a living, taking care of our families, and enjoying the blessings of this physical life. There's everything wrong with letting these things replace God and his Kingdom. Not only can these "good" things interfere with your spiritual progress, but you can also get yourself caught in a disaster having done nothing to protect yourself. You will be destroyed too, along with the rest of the world, just because you wanted to enjoy life.

Jesus rebuked the Pharisees for being so obsessed over unimportant details and missing the great matters of the soul.

> Woe to you, teachers of the Law and Pharisees, you hypocrites! You give a tenth of your spices – mint, dill and cummin. But you have neglected the more important matters of the Law – justice, mercy and faithfulness. You should have practiced the latter, without neglecting the former. You blind guides! You strain out a gnat but swallow a camel. (Matthew 23:23-24)

They were so preoccupied with trivial details of the Law that they didn't seem to realize they were disqualified for Heaven. This is a fatal characteristic of legalists; we have our own versions of them in our day.

You can even make this mistake with otherwise permissible affairs of life. When Jesus visited Martha and Mary, Martha was upset with her sister because she needed help in the kitchen to get the meal ready, and there was Mary "irresponsibly" sitting at Jesus' feet learning instead.

> But Martha was distracted by all the preparations that had to be made. She came to him and asked, "Lord, don't you care that my sister has left me to do the work by myself? Tell her to help me!" "Martha, Martha," the Lord answered, "you are worried and upset about many things, but only one thing is needed. Mary has chosen what is better, and it will not be taken away from her." (Luke 10:40-42)

You're not going to get Jesus on your side if you want to justify your "busy-ness" in the affairs of life. Jesus wouldn't have cared if there wasn't any meal that day, if he could spend his time leading these women in the way of life instead.

Time is short. Not only do we not know when the Lord is coming back (the book of Revelation says that it's soon!), we don't know when our time will come to go to him. We ought to live as if this is our last day; what have we not yet done to prepare for that day? Again, Jesus shows us an example with a man too busy with the affairs of this life to tend to his soul.

> The ground of a certain rich man produced a good crop. He thought to himself, 'What shall I do? I have no place to store my crops.' Then he said, 'This is what I'll do. I will tear down my barns and build bigger ones, and there I will store all my grain and my goods. And I'll say to myself, "You have plenty of good things laid up for many years. Take life easy; eat, drink and be merry."' But God said to him, 'You fool! This very night your life will be demanded from you. Then who will get what you have prepared for yourself?' This is how it will be with anyone who stores up things for himself but is not rich toward God. (Luke 12:16-21)

What a tragic mistake! Even making a living can choke out our spiritual focus. We will never survive spiritually if our hearts are so focused on things of this world. Notice what Jesus said about people's perfectly harmless activities in the days of Noah.

> As it was in the days of Noah, so it will be at the coming of the Son of Man. For in the days before the flood, people were eating and drinking, marrying and giving in marriage, up to the day Noah entered the ark; and they knew nothing about what would happen until the flood came and took them all away. That is how it will be at the coming of the Son of Man. (Matthew 24:37-39)

A person with wisdom, who is living by faith, will realize that God is building a spiritual Kingdom; it is only a matter of time till he destroys this world, and only that eternal Kingdom will be left. The survivor will have certain priorities in his life to make sure he lives through that great transition at the end of time.

- **Habitual lifestyle** – It isn't enough to do what God says once, and then sit back on your laurels and wait for rewards. God expects you to do it tomorrow too, and the next day, and the next. Don't bother looking for the rewards, because you still haven't done anything impressive yet. There have been many "Christians" who started out well, and then over a long period of time they fell away from God and left the faith.

> Let us not become weary in doing good, for at the proper time we will reap a harvest if we do not give up. (Galatians 6:9)

Jesus told the story about the servant who did what he was told, and was then expected to do more – without praise.

> Suppose one of you had a servant plowing or looking after the sheep. Would he say to the servant when he comes in from the field, 'Come along now and sit down to eat'? Would he not rather say, 'Prepare my supper, get yourself ready and wait on me while I eat and drink; after that you may eat and drink'? Would he thank the servant because he did what he was told to do? So you also, when you have done everything you were told to do, should say, 'We are unworthy servants; we have only done our duty.' (Luke 17:7-10)

He isn't being harsh, he just knows what we're like. When we do something right, we tend to look around expecting the music to play and someone to hand out the medals, like the Pharisees praying in public for all to see. The faithful, plodding servant who does his duty day in and day out is worth much more to him than the glory-seeker. When you faithfully perform your service to him when nobody is looking, when there are no paychecks involved, and in fact when the circumstances make it hard to do that duty – that's what impresses him, especially when he finds you still at it long after he assigned it to you. Then it's obvious that you believe in his cause and will see it through to the end no matter what.

- **Simplicity of a child** – A child is naturally trusting. He or she believes whatever their parents tell them. The world is still simple to them; don't confuse them with the complexities of the deceitful world of adults. They willingly follow adults, assuming that adults know what they're doing. They know they can't live without the help of an adult.

Our religion, Jesus told us, should be that simple and childlike. Jesus appreciated children for that reason; he counseled us to emulate them.

> I tell you the truth, unless you change and become like little children, you will never enter the kingdom of Heaven. (Matthew 18:3)

God is our Father, and he knows what he's doing; so whatever he tells you is right. Believe him. Do what he commands. Trust him as he leads you by the hand. Don't try to figure this out on your own, or try your own solutions. Just accept everything from his hand and don't question him or make things difficult.

Try teaching a children's Sunday School class sometime. You have to make it simple so that they can understand it. You have to be honest and straightforward with them: they want to hear about miracles, and believing in God's promises, and being good in all ways. Then go home and hang your head in shame, because you don't believe or live even half of what you tell these children in their simplicity. Adults have built so many layers of deceit, excuses and duplicity into their lives, even into their Christianity, that they have lost that simple faith in Jesus that children are so good at. Jesus shakes his head over us because of how complicated and dishonest we've become in our religion.

> The Pharisees … you must obey them and do everything they tell you. But do not do what they do, for they do not practice what they preach. (Matthew 23:3)

The point is this: remember the great principles of the faith. God really does do miracles; wait on them. God is utterly holy and righteous; he expects the same from you, nothing less. God hates this world of sin; he doesn't want to see you playing around with it. God promised that he will hold you up and protect you; don't fear anything or anybody. The Bible is simple and plain in what it teaches; believe it.

- **Fruit of the Spirit** – As we are naturally, we don't have much going for us if our goal is to be with God. We are sinners at best, and even Christians struggle with the "old man" that wants to keep dragging us back to the world.

> Can the Ethiopian change his skin or the leopard its spots? Neither can you do good who are accustomed to doing evil. (Jeremiah 13:23)

We've already seen that it's going to take a great deal of training and work to become more like Christ. One thing that we do have going for us, however, is that we have the Spirit of Christ in us, guiding us and pushing us along in the right direction.

Just remember what the Spirit's job is: he is molding us and changing us to make us look like Jesus. Not physically but spiritually. Otherwise, God the Father wouldn't be interested in having us around in Heaven.

> And we, who with unveiled faces all reflect the Lord's glory, are being transformed into his likeness with ever-increasing glory, which comes from the Lord, who is the Spirit. (2 Corinthians 3:18)

So, what *does* Jesus look like spiritually?

But the fruit of the Spirit is love, joy, peace, patience, kindness, goodness, faithfulness, gentleness and self-control. Against such things there is no law. Those who belong to Christ Jesus have crucified the sinful nature with its passions and desires. (Galatians 5:22-24)

Now when God applies the fires of affliction and hardship to a person's life, *this* is what he wants to see come out of them. He doesn't want to see trash (anger, wrath, lust, stealing, adultery, dissensions, rebellion – all the works of the sinful flesh), but rather the righteousness of Christ. It's like squeezing grapes to get wine; he doesn't want to get sour, rotten juice!

Keep in mind, then, that hard times and trials are processes that God uses to test your worth. He wants to bring your heart out into the open, and make it plain to everyone whether or not you are a *nice person,* even under pressure. If you're nice to people even when life is a burden, then your heart must be pure and holy. However, if pressure makes you unbearable to be around, that's proof that your heart isn't as good as you claim that it is. Jesus said it best.

For from within, out of men's hearts, come evil thoughts, sexual immorality, theft, murder, adultery, greed, malice, deceit, lewdness, envy, slander, arrogance and folly. All these evils come from inside and make a man 'unclean.' (Mark 7:21-23)

The goal is always, *always* to make you ready to live with God in Heaven. Stick to the Mission; follow the leading of the Spirit. Don't be satisfied with yourself until you look and act like Christ in all circumstances.

Stay with God

We mentioned before that holiness means being God-centered in your whole life. Whatever you do, whatever you say, act as if you're standing in front of God when you do and say those things – because you really are! Your place now, since you've been called to be holy, is before his throne. The whole purpose of giving us his Spirit was so that you can stay with him.

This is the secret of survival. God will understand if you aren't strong and wise; you will change over time as he works with you. You could be utterly helpless, and yet he is committed to making sure you are protected and cared for. He is the Rock, the strong place, the fortress, the wise Creator, the Redeemer, the Bread from Heaven, the Light that shines our way. Rest in him, weak as you are, and you will make it.

> He lifted me out of the slimy pit, out of the mud and mire; he set my feet on a rock and gave me a firm place to stand. (Psalm 40:2)

You may be as helpless and weak as a bruised reed, but when the reed rests on the Rock, it can't be moved. Spiritual survival requires spiritual stamina, not physical prowess. That's why women and children, who are weaker than men physically, can survive hardship just as well as (and often better than) men, who often rely on their own prowess and resources. It requires faith, not genius; it requires humility, not pride; it requires the Spirit, not natural skills.

And when you spend time with God, you will learn that he doesn't like to stand still. He has a lot to do in your life. He's always on the move. You are going to be busy working on all sorts of issues that will take up a great deal of your time and energy. Since very few people around you are going to be so intense in their faith, you'll have to learn to strike out on your own. God isn't going to wait for them, and he doesn't want you hanging back there either. It's time to learn self-discipline and follow God as he leads you into spiritual maturity.

You have started on a journey. Pack up your bags, follow the Spirit, and move on to your eternal home.

Conclusion

Unfortunately, the only good way that you can tell if someone is prepared for the future is when the future finally arrives. Nobody really knows how they will react in times of trouble.

But we can tell if you have any wisdom *now*. The wise man heeds a warning; and Jesus has given us a solemn warning about how this world works. It's broken, things don't work the way that they're supposed to, and you *are* going to have trouble with it. Jesus ought to know! The wise man turns to God for the *right kind* of help to get him through this world into Heaven. Only Christ's path leads to Heaven.

> The way of a fool seems right to him, but a wise man listens to advice. (Proverbs 12:15)

When Moses led the Israelites out of Egypt, he took them to the edge of the Red Sea. Pharaoh and the Egyptians thought for sure that the Israelites were trapped, and that it would be an easy matter to beat them and drag them back to slavery. In fact, the Israelites themselves were very discouraged about the situation; they didn't see any way out of this dilemma.

Moses, however, was a survivor. He knew God's ways; he had been personally trained by God to handle difficult situations. Now the time had come to make survivors out of the Israelites.

> Do not be afraid. Stand firm and you will see the deliverance the LORD will bring you today. The Egyptians you see today you will never see again. The LORD will fight for you; you need only to be still. (Exodus 14:13-14)

What did they learn that day? To trust in God alone; this is the secret to spiritual survival.

> Your path led through the sea, your way through the mighty waters, though your footprints were not seen. (Psalm 77:19)

Conclusion

God leads us *through* this world, as impossible as it may seem, to the spiritual home that he has prepared for us in glory. So, like the Israelites, let's put on a survivor's character and endure the hardship of the journey, so that we can enjoy the reward of the faithful.

> If they had been thinking of the country they had left, they would have had opportunity to return. Instead, they were longing for a better country – a Heavenly one. Therefore God is not ashamed to be called their God, for he has prepared a city for them. (Hebrews 11:15-16)

Subject Index

Index

Index

Scripture Index

Index

Index

Index

Notes

Notes

Books available from

Ravenbrook Publishers

Mystery Revealed: A Beginner's Bible Survey   *(424 pages, $25)*

This Survey takes the student through the entire Bible – first with an analysis of the whole Bible, then looking at the major divisions of the Bible and how they contribute to the whole picture.

Eight Fundamentals of the Christian Faith   *(361 pages, $15)*

According to Hebrews, each believer should be thoroughly familiar with the basics of the faith, so much so that you can teach others. This is an in-depth study of each of the basics mentioned in Hebrews.

Jesus and the New Testament   *(349 pages, $15)*

The New Testament is made up of two things: the story of Jesus' life on earth, and the Apostles' testimony of his unique nature and work. The result is a living fulfillment of God's project of salvation that was first worked out in the Old Testament.

Where the Paths Meet   *(269 pages, $15)*

This book focuses on the major aspects of both Old and New Testaments to show how the entire Bible forms one story, one way of salvation, one road to God.

Ten Keys to the Bible   *(591 pages, $15)*

There are certain "keys" that the student needs to learn for studying the Bible. Master these Keys, and you will be better equipped to unlock any passage of the Bible and find its true meaning

The Witness   *(258 pages, $15)*

God wisely arranged the Bible as a collection of affidavits of eyewitnesses who can testify to the reality and works of God. These witnesses have given us a written record of God that makes the Bible a bastion of truth that gives comfort to the saints and gives the church the foundation it needs to stand against attacks from the Enemy.

The Works of the Lord   *(345 pages, $15)*

There are certain works that only God can do. The first order of business for every Christian is to find out what God's works are – not only to give us the agenda for our prayers, but also to teach us what to wait for. In wisdom we won't try to do God's works, but we will wait on God for what only he can do.

A Bible Catechism   *(146 pages, $15)*

One of the best ways to learn the major doctrines of our faith is by question and answer. This book teaches the student about the basics of Christianity through easy-to-understand answers to questions that even children can understand.

The Bible Explains Creation   *(293 pages, $15)*

The Bible gives us a fuller description of how God created the universe than science can ever give us. But you have to use the entire Bible, from Genesis to Revelation, to see the spiritual framework that supports our physical world.

Glory: The Holiness of God and Man   *(122 pages, $15)*

Man was created to know and enjoy God – this is the definition of holiness. Sin separated us from God; so the work of Christ is to restore that relationship and lift man up to a higher level than we thought imaginable – to know God *as Jesus knows him*.

A Holy Temple   *(198 pages, $15)*

The church was designed to be a formidable force in our society; unfortunately in our day it's become weak and ineffective. This book explores a number of areas that will strengthen the testimony and work of a church to give it the truth and power that modern man needs.

Knots Untied   *(229 pages, $15)*

There are certain issues in the Bible that, on the surface, look simple enough to understand – until you begin asking some probing questions. **Knots Untied** examines a few of these issues and finds some surprising answers.

The Measure of a Christian   *(247 pages, $15)*

The Measure of a Christian looks at the root issues of living the Christian life. What are the marks of a true Christian? What kind of church does a Christian need to grow spiritually? How important is discipline to a person's life? How does God discipline his children?

A New Model for Biblical Studies   *(59 pages, $12)*

The traditional way of looking at the Bible, unfortunately, has robbed us of its richness and usability. In this book we take a slightly different approach and find not only the treasure chest of the Old Testament opening up to us, but a clear picture of how it unfolds into the New Testament.

No Proof Needed   *(83 pages, $12)*

Men and nations have attacked the Bible for thousands of years, but it still reveals the truth about God and man in spite of the attacks. If we understand the wisdom behind the making of the Bible, we will see that God doesn't need our efforts to prove its truth – it stands on its own.

The Secret to Answered Prayer   *(188 pages, $15)*

The Bible is very specific about how one must approach God. In this book we learn six principles to keep in mind if one wants answers from the God of the Bible.

Profitable Servants   *(113 pages, $15)*

Jesus taught about the "unprofitable servant" to impress on us the many duties that he holds us all responsible for. Even one talent is more than you might think! This book explores the responsibilities that the Lord has given his people.

Teaching Children About Jesus   *(324 pages, $15)*

Children will believe anything you teach them. That's why it's vitally important to get as much of the truth into their heads as you can while they are still open to it. Here we look at what you must teach about Jesus, and the message of the Bible, to lay a good foundation for their future.

The Throne of David   *(159 pages, $15)*

David pulled the nation of Israel together according to a five-point plan, around a Mission that brought the people back to God. Jesus, as the Son of David, builds his church according to the same plan. We need to learn that plan so that we can work with him, not against him, in our churches.

Tools for Bible Teachers   *(79 pages, $12)*

Being a Bible teacher requires some important skills and resources; not every volunteer in church can do the job as God requires. This is an overview of what those skills are; with them, you can successfully teach the Bible to your students.

The *Treasury of Christ* Commentary of the Bible

This commentary focuses on bringing out the important points that a Christian needs for his spiritual faith and walk with God, book by book.

Completed volumes:

Volume 1: Overview of the Old Testament (190 pages, $15)

Check with Ravenbrook for additional titles.

Removing the Veil   *(151 pages, $15)*

Moses had to put a covering over his head to hide the Glory of God, which symbolized the fact that the Jews didn't understand the spiritual meanings behind the elements of their religion. Jesus removes that veil for Christians. This book explores the main themes of the Old Testament in an easy-to-read presentation, so that the Christian can understand why the Old Testament is so crucial for one's faith.

Words of Gold   *(187 pages, $25)*

Many Christians have never been taught how to study the Bible. Here the student is introduced to the tools of Bible study, with numerous examples and homework.

A Manual for Spiritual Survival   *(203 pages, $15)*

The modern church is in more of an entertainment mode than set up for training. But hard times will come upon every one of us, in some form. In this book we look at specific areas, for both the church and the individual Christian, to help them become survivors and to prepare for hardship and trial.

The Ways of the Lord   *(199 pages, $15)*

The entire Bible teaches us that the Lord has ways of doing things. In Hebrews we read that the Israelites failed to learn those ways – which is why God refused to let them into the Promised Land. Christians also need to learn his ways if they want to enter Heaven.

What the Bible Says About Hell   *(100 pages, $15)*

Hell is not what many people think it is. Here we learn exactly what Hell is like, and who will go there. Also covered are the many myths of Hell that confuse so many people, and what the Bible really says about these issues.

You can order these books on-line at this website:

www. shenbible.org

Or you can send a check or money order (US Funds) to this address:

Ravenbrook Publishers
PO Box 103
Weyers Cave, VA 24486

Costs include shipping to US locations only; check with Ravenbrook for overseas shipping costs.
Be sure to include your shipping address.

www.ingramcontent.com/pod-product-compliance
Lightning Source LLC
Chambersburg PA
CBHW021052090426
42738CB00006B/299